186251

# Utopian Literature

Advisory Editor:
*ARTHUR ORCUTT LEWIS, JR.*
*Professor of English*
The Pennsylvania State University

# Looking Backward And What I Saw

*W. W. Satterlee*

Introduction by *Arthur O. Lewis, Jr.*

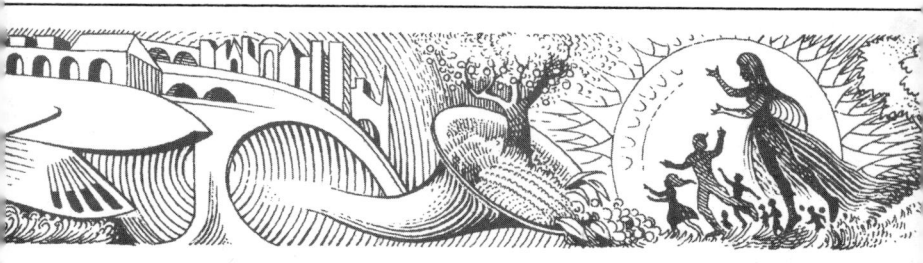

ARNO PRESS & THE NEW YORK TIMES
NEW YORK · 1971

PN
3448
U7 S3

Reprint Edition 1971 by Arno Press Inc.
Introduction Copyright 1971 by Arno Press Inc.

Reprinted from a copy in The Pennsylvania State University Library

LC# 76-154461
ISBN 0-405-03543-8

Utopian Literature
ISBN for complete set: 0-405-03510-1

Manufactured in the United States of America

Publisher's Note: This edition was reprinted from the best available copy

# INTRODUCTION

IT IS CERTAINLY NOT FOR ITS LITERARY MERIT ALONE that one would read *Looking Backward and What I Saw*, and, despite its publication in at least two editions, few have read it for any other reason. Nevertheless, there is good cause to examine this work, not only for its criticism of utopian ideals of the late nineteenth century, but also for its proposal of a utopia. Satterlee saw grave danger in Henry George's Single Tax, in Edward Bellamy's Industrial Army, and in a number of other related reform schemes. When one adds to these concerns his further fear of the problems arising from drinking and falling away from Christianity, it is easy to see why this Professor of Political Science and Hygienic Philosophy at U.S. Grant University would write as he did. As he put it, "This work is contributed to the amount already written and spoken by others, that there may be no lack of warning to the citizens of our beloved country, not to be lead [sic] astray by blind leaders, lest the pit of destruction should suddenly open and swallow them up."

The plot of Satterlee's book is the familiar one in which the narrator—in this case Mr. R. E. Former—dreams of the future and then awakens to write his book. Mr. Former describes himself as one who has moved up from the very poorest of origins, "A radical by birth and early association," and has become concerned with the future of his family if he were to die; it is this concern that leads him to his adventure.

Setting the tone of the book are the words he hears in his reverie just before the dream begins: "Seek ye first the kingdom of God." Throughout the dream Former uses his Christian ideals as a touchstone against which to test the information he obtains. Not unexpectedly the influence of John Bunyan and other Christian allegorists is obvious both in the contents of the dreams within the dream and in the names of persons and places throughout the book.

In his dream Former becomes a guest at the Palace Heartway of Mr. Right Pathfinder and his wife and remains under their tutelage throughout. As the story progresses he obtains information about the future world from three chief sources: from discussions with the friendly and sympathetic Mr. Pathfinder, from reading in the Pathfinder library, and from a personal tour of the country. Satterlee's version of the future-society dream includes the further device of having the narrator dream—or at least see fantastic visions—on a number of occasions, and each of these visions or dreams within a dream serves as commentary on the evil to come if the nation follows the path which has lately "set the restless masses all agog."

Each dream develops logically from and serves as commentary on the preceding discussion. As he learns more about the past two hundred years, Former's fears move from generalized to specific, from mild concern to real fright. The first vision of literary celebrities, with special notice to Edward Bellamy and Henry George, and the dream of social reformers playing leapfrog are simple commentary on the hypocrisy, futility, and—as the conversion to donkeys indicates—stupidity of their schemes. Up to this point Former has learned little beyond the fact that he has somehow been moved to January 1, 2101, but the more alarming information which follows produces more intense and unpleasant stirrings of his subconscious mind

Following Pathfinder's description of the downfall of the United States—the result of the same influences Satterlee feared in 1890: unlimited immigration, slackening of religious observances, formation of secret societies, and, above all, "the alcoholic liquor traffic"—Former's dream of the Working Man's Pond becomes a discouraging parable of the manner in which vested interests prevent true reform. After he learns about the "utopia" which followed the fall of the United States, his dream of the pneumatic tube, "Socialism," and its corollary devices is a graphic representation of his fear that individual men will count for nothing in the coming society. The final dream, following perusal of the record of the Convention of 1987 and triggered by the low level of acceptance of churchgoing in the twenty-second century, strikes at the heart of Former's religious beliefs. The possibility demonstrated by the dream that the direction society is taking may prevent his achieving Heaven is his most fearsome dream. There are no more dreams within the dream, only the ever more frightening experiences which culminate in the death of Pathfinder and Former's awakening, back in 1890.

In his discussions with Mr. Pathfinder, Former has learned something of the way in which social, economic, and political conditions already obvious in 1890 have moved to their logical conclusion: the single tax experiment, followed by civil war, and eventually, following the Convention of 1987, to a socialist utopia. His reading of General Dick Tator's message to the Convention and of some of the speeches made by delegates permits Satterlee to describe and criticize several reform ideas—those of the "blind leaders" of his own time—and to present one of his own.

General Tator's proposals are intended "to avoid if possible the evils which attended the career of the old Republic." For him these evils "were concentrated in the intense individualism, and social antagonisms, arising from the personal liberty, and public freedom of its citizens." His plan would destroy acquisitiveness on the part of mankind and "establish a perfect and universal equipoise between vice and virtue." His scheme is a variation on that of Bellamy, including education of children by the government and of purely secular character; universal service in the industrial army till retirement at age 45 "with a life annuity to be paid from the nation's goods" (there is an option to retire on half pension at age 33); non-transferable credit cards representing the individual's share of the national productivity; universal male suffrage at age 45; all land, including that confiscated from foreigners, held by the government; government ownership and operation of public utilities; marriages as "civil contract binding only at the will of both parties, and to be severed at the will of those who make it." Cooperation of the industrial army will lead to increased production, and, the General proposes, "The government should manufacture whatever is demanded by any considerable number of people. The personal habits of the people must be held sacred and therefore opium, tobacco, and liquors should be furnished as freely as food and clothing. The aim of the government should be to develop the virtue and power of the people by gratifying all their possible wants, and by permitting no competitions in business, destroy all possible antagonisms among men." There will be no courts or lawyers because all disputes will be settled by arbitration between man and man, and, with all wants satisfied, there will be no incentive for crime. The army and navy will be unnecessary because the nations of the world, having adopted similar plans, will not want to fight anymore.

Although General Tator's plan is to be the chief object of criticism, Satterlee devotes almost twenty pages to Former's reading of speeches by other delegates. These delegates, aptly named to emphasize their theses, present agreement with and variations from the General's plan, and by doing so, demonstrate why his is so plausible a solution to the problem at hand. Under the circumstances it is logical that the last speaker, the Honorable Moses Heartway, should concentrate his attack on his Bellamy-like proposal.

Heartway, for whom Pathfinder has named his home, is represented in Pathfinder's library by a well-worn volume containing his Convention speech as well as the general outline of his teachings on social problems. Former does not use the Convention record in this case, but rather listens as Pathfinder reads to him from Heartway's book. A brief examination of his attack on General Dick Tator's proposals is therefore of some interest in understanding Satterlee's criticism of "this deceptive phantom."

The arguments against Tator-Bellamy are generally the same as those put forth by other anti-Bellamy writers such as Arthur D. Vinton (*Look-*

*ing Further Backward,* 1890), Richard Michaelis (*Looking Further Forward,* 1890), and J. W. Roberts (*Looking Within,* 1893). Like Roberts, Satterlee uses the occasion to describe his own utopian ideal. As is usually the case, the main attack is on the belief in the natural goodness of man: "It is the main fault of this as of all other forms of socialism, that it ignores the fact of the natural depravity of the race, provides no adequate remedy for the disease of sin, and in every tenet denies the law of man's being which makes adversity a developing power, and antagonisms the rungs in the ladder of human endeavor, which aid in lifting him to the highest possibilities of his manhood." Good intentions and abundant material possessions for the asking will not lessen the need for laws and moral teachings. "We cannot make good citizens," says Heartway, "with a motherless childhood, a Godless youth, and a manhood that knows but one incentive to action, the feeding and clothing of this physical organism."

Heartway goes on to point out the ways in which various aspects of Dick Tator's plan would lead to greater evils than those which it proposed to cure. Thus, the credit check would lead to counterfeiting; early retirement would create a huge body of idlers; the lack of a standing army would permit unlimited immigration; the provision for public entertainment and dispensation of liquor, opium, and tobacco would reduce incentive to work; the demands of the industrial army would break up the family. Furthermore, he argues, the system is economically unsound, for it would lead to hatred of hard work, eliminate incentive to produce effectively, reduce the labor force drastically, limit the opportunity for advancement to those least qualified, and isolate the nation from the rest of the world. He concludes that General Dick Tator's scheme has "sincerity of purpose," but its adoption would bring about even greater disaster than that already suffered. Events during Satterlee's visit in 2101 prove him right.

Moses Heartway's own "more excellent way" is described in the volume of his writings from which Pathfinder reads. A number of almost aphoristic sayings preface the report of his speech at the Convention. They reinforce his criticism and form the basis for his reforms. One can scarcely quarrel with such beliefs as: "True personal liberty lies within the circle of the law"; "that natural tendency toward evil in man cannot be corrected by satisfying his natural wants"; "we may not lose our individualism in marching columns or masses"; "woman as well as man, withers and dwarfs, when restricted to a narrower limit than that of her natural possibilities"; "a permanent social order cannot be built on the ruins of another"; and, most significant of all, "to have a new and better social order we must have new men. Men ought to be made new by the way of the heart, not by the way of their environment."

Based on these principles, Heartway's reforms include proposals typical of the late nineteenth century. Thus, he calls for restriction of ownership of land; taxation following equitable assessment; universal male and female suffrage (with exceptions for those who have committed a crime, foreigners, and illiterates); direct election of all officers of the government by secret ballot; creation of larger divisions than the old states; a small standing army made up of state-supported militia, free compulsory education, both secular and moral, with the Bible used as a textbook in every school ("No system of education, no form of government, can be made conducive to the good of mankind, which does not provide for the development and control of his religious nature"); eight-hour working day with wages fixed by a National Bureau of Work and Wages; banning of monopolies; limited immigration; and, as might be expected from one who believes as Satterlee did, emphasis on the Sabbath; strengthening of family relationships; repeal of all divorce laws; and, most of all, banning of the sale and use of all alcoholic beverages. Had the American republic not fallen to drinking, "the Nation's curse," all would have been well, and Heartway proposes that a return to this model, correcting its errors, is the best possibility. He concludes, "Let us first of all acknowledge God, the Supreme Ruler and Governor of all things, then let us make our social system conform to His law, and thereby all may be attained which is possible under our present state."

Satterlee has performed the good critic's function. He has presented the case for the opposition, shown its deficiencies, and then offered a remedy of his own. He has been honest with the opposition, for everywhere he gives credit for the sincerity of those proposing the schemes he dislikes. Thus, in the preface his chief charge against "the would-be social reformers" is "mistaking cause for effect." General Dick Tator might have made himself a king or even a tyrant and did not. He is hailed as a "great leader," and the men at the Convention are described as "distinguished statesmen." Nevertheless, good intentions are not enough, and these men have been the "blind leaders" whose influence led Satterlee to write his book. Adoption of Dick Tator's "nationalistic, social and revolutionary scheme" has brought about the society in which the Pathfinders live. The dire warnings of Heartway have come true, and the end of Former's dream is the burning of the city of Bellamy in the revolution which attempts to overthrow the now-impossible government.

But what about the society Satterlee advocates? Excellent as it is on the surface, many modern readers would find it unacceptable, for it would produce a society in which not all men would share alike. This outcome is made clear in part by the Reverend Go-The-Old-Way's sermon but chiefly by Former's personal experience. Upon starting out on his journey through the land, Former notices a cat eating the rats near the barn, a hawk pursuing small birds, big fish eating little fish, "regardless of . . . the possible ties of consanguinity," and some trees still standing in the midst of others which have been uprooted. Such occurrences, he believes, are God's will: "Thus I saw this law, this inexorable law written in everything about me, 'the survival of the fittest.'" The behavior of most of the people he sees on his journey bears out this observation, for they do not hesitate to take advantage of those who are weaker. Since Heartway's proposal, as well as those he has opposed, assumes that somehow man will be made better—Heartway, through the teachings of Christianity, his opponents through satisfaction of man's physical wants—God's will, the survival of the fittest, would seem to insure that neither system can be made to benefit all men. Former awakens from his "horrid nightmare" leaving the reader with a sense that perhaps not even the best possible reforms can really improve the lot of mankind short of the Promised Land. It is not Edward Bellamy's, or Henry George's, or Dick Tator's, or Moses Heartway's, but "God's social order" that must prevail, and, as Go-The-Old-Way had pointed out, "In his rewards and punishments God makes distinctions in men." Although, in the end, it may bring about "the perfection of species and the maintenance of the standard" called for in the sermon, no society constructed on such principles will provide for the good of all men. Utopia, in other words, must be purchased, even according to divine will, at the expense of others. Most social reformers have not subscribed to this view. But, after all, it was his concern for the influence of these "blind leaders" that caused Satterlee to write his book.

ARTHUR O. LEWIS<br>MAY 1971

# Looking Backward;

### AND

# WHAT I SAW.

**BY**

**W. W. SATTERLEE,**

Chair of Political Science and Hygienic Philosophy,

U. S. Grant University.

1890-2101.

Entered according to act of Congress in the year 1890, by W. W. Satterlee, in the office of the Librarian of Congress, at Washington.

**All Rights Reserved.**

HARRISON & SMITH,
MINNEAPOLIS.

# DEDICATION.

To my sincere and valued friends and co-laborers in moral reform, in the City of Minneapolis and in the state of "Sky-Tinted Waters," who have faltered not when honest conviction led in the unequal contest, is this humble effort to further their cause most affectionately dedicated by,

The Author.

# PREFACE.

One need not make apology for calling the attention of his countrymen, to the live questions now agitating the minds and hearts of the thinking men and women of all nations. Rather he would be an enemy to his race, who, seeing the danger, should fail to sound a note of warning, simply because in the eyes of some, "his bodily presence was weak and his speech contemptible."

The author invites candid judgment on what he brings to the literary market, rather than on the vehicle which for the time being affords it means of transportation.

The hands alike of rich and poor are stretched out toward the future, and their eyes are filled with painful anxiety as they watch and wait for the dawning of the better days. This is humanity's unerring tribute to the story of the fall, and of the promised restoration.

Such anxious hearts are liable to be deceived by the "Lo, here is Christ," of the would be social reformers, who, mistaking cause for effect, would reverse the order of nature and make the fountain pure by cleansing the stream.

When a purely ideal, and necessarily impossible scheme of social order, in itself but "the baseless fabric of a vision," is able, as of late, to set the restless masses all agog; and when thousands mentally leaping over every obstruction of nature, fact and logic, grasp at this phantom as something real to be pratically applied to human society, is it not time for fear?

Is it not the duty of toiling and thinking men, who would begin at the heart to develop the man, to seize the hard cold facts of human life and hurl them at this deceptive phantom, lest men in their distraction forget God, law, and human rights together?

The author from the practical standpoint of a laboring man believes that evolution in the present state of society is better than revolution. If what we could do were done, the visionary part of socialism, would either drop to realism, or vanish from sight forever.

If the billions squandered on drink, tobacco and useless display were saved, seven tenths of the "cry for bread" would be hushed. If the burdened masses will not do this, then the battle cry should be "millions for christian and temperance evangelization, but not a cent for the Devil's tribute."

If money is to be spent as millions of our people spend it, then the divine arrangement by which wealth is attainable only by temperance and toil, by frugality and economy, is of all our blessings the greatest. In the use of money it is not how much we spend that brings blessing, but *how* we spend.

This work is contributed to the amount already written and spoken by others, that there may be no lack of warning to the citizens of our beloved country, not to be lead astray by blind leaders, lest the pit of destruction should suddenly open and swallow them up.  THE AUTHOR.

Minneapolis, June 20th, 1890.

# LOOKING BACKWARD;
# AND WHAT I SAW.

### CHAPTER I.

God's hand had gently drawn the curtains of the night, thus shutting in from a universe of cares and fears his children; when weary and sad I laid me down to rest. The day had been full of anxious thought, concerning the social problems which were agitating the minds of my countrymen, and I retired sick at heart, over "man's inhumanity to man."

For a long time drowsily I mused on the varied incidents of my life, which had been one of toil, both physical, and mental, from my boyhood. I had never been able to make provision for life's necessities beyond the passing day, and having at my fireside a round half dozen of boys and girls to feed, clothe, and educate; and with their patient and loving mother's assistance to rear to manhood, and womanhood; mine had been a life of anxiety and care.

In my early years a tiller of the soil, a day laborer for wages, a companion of the poor, and an associate of the lowly; and farther on in life a professional man, burdened with the sorrows and needs of others outside the family circle, I had obtained a varied experience in the practical things of life, which in some degree made amends for my lack of opportunity to obtain more than the most common, of a common school education. A radical by birth and early association, I had freely espoused the cause of the poor and downtrodden, making their cause my own and their uplifting my highest aim.

While thus dreamily I lay contemplating the past, life's lights and shadows seemed to rise, and fall, until my passions were stirred to their profoundest depths. There came unbidden from the distant past, the memories of the trials I had known, the constant struggle for a bare existence; the pity or scorn of the rich, the ungratefulness of the poor, the inequalities in human lives; until my soul in very frenzy by its own communings uttered with inexpressible anguish the old, old cry of doubt and despair; "How doth God know? and is there knowledge in the Most High?" "Verily I have cleansed my heart in vain, and washed my hands in innocency. For all the day long have I been plagued, and chastened every morning."

Then came flocking in, a troop of forebodings for the future. I felt that old age was coming on, life's forces were giving way, and I had nothing laid up for "the rainy day." If suddenly I should be called to die, my family would be cast on the cold charities of a self-seeking world. And but little would the people of such a world remember of the deeds of kindness performed in their behalf by the husband, and father, whose voice was now stilled in death; that they might requite them to his dependent loved ones But suddenly breaking into the bitterness of my reverie there came a voice not unfamiliar to my soul, which, in accents sweet as music, and loving as a mother's croning to her babe, questioned my inmost being.

"Why do you murmur? You say you have lived by the day, but has not the day's supply been sufficient? Have you or yours ever felt hunger unappeased, or needed warmth which was unprovided? Have your children cried for bread or have you been obliged to turn the stranger from your door because you had nothing to share with him? Have I not been faithful to my promise, 'Trust in the Lord and do good, and verily thou shalt be fed?'" Confusion and shame took possession of my being, as I confessed the injustice of my murmurings; then leaning my soul far out to listen, that I might catch the last and faintest accents of that voice, I heard as it died away in sweet cadences this; only this. "Seek ye first the kingdom of God and his righteousness; and all these things shall be added unto you." Resting as trustingly as a child does on the bosom of its mother, I fell asleep.

I slept and dreamed. I thought myself moving through space in that indescribable Dream-land way, in which one flies without the impediment of wings, and without fear or exertion. I seemed to be passing over a land of wondrous beauty, endowed by nature with all graces. Mountains and hills stretched far away, with wide and luxuriant valleys between them. In parts vast plains were seen, while here and there small streams or mighty rivers coursed their way to the ocean. Beautiful lakes like inland seas added their utility, while great forests tossed their branches as if to welcome me to their shades.

Somehow it seemed to me in my dream that this was my native country, my own loved America; and yet as now and then my flight brought me close to the surface, as I skimmed along as does a swallow at evening tide; I thought I could discern changes most remarkable in the condition of the country, as it appeared quite unlike that to which I had been accustomed in my travels. Large farms were overgrown with grass and weeds, the fences decayed or gone, the houses and barns tottering to their fall; while marks of unthrift appeared on every hand.

As I passed over hamlets and villages, or poised in my exhilerating flight over great cities, I could but observe that ruin, destruction and decay were everywhere apparent. I saw immense structures which in comparison with others about them, appeared to me like the remains of a former more notable civilization. But they were crumbling back to dust. Great factories, whose wheels were once whirring out their mission of blessing to mankind, were still as the voice of death. Some old churches, here and there, seemed to have withstood the shocks of time, and of the elements; but their doors were shut forever. Their entrances were overgrown with vines and trees, so dense as to make ingress or egress, quite impossible.

In the market places the people idled. Apparently at great expense, parks, sporting grounds, and race courses had been fitted up. Here I saw large congregations of people, men, women, and children; who shouted and jeered, while fiery steeds speeded on the track, or bulls tossed their human antagonists; while various kinds of beasts struggled with men, in the great arenas for mastery. My heart sickened at the sight of these brutalities, but when I observed further, that thousands of these people were besotted with wine, and that the drink houses were open on every hand I turned away, my heart burning with sorrow and shame. I observed as I passed along that great lines of railway had fallen into disuse, and scarcely a steamer could I see upon the great rivers. Certainly I thought if this be my country, it must be relapsing into Pagan Barbarism.

Suddenly I found myself moving along the coast line of an ocean and a great maratime bay lay at my feet. I looked out over the rolling blue waters of the harbor for a sail, but I looked in vain; while the old hulks that rotted along the shore presented an object history which could not be misunderstood. Every where desolation reigned. The inhabitants seemed to have lost all ambition, and a generation of beggars had taken possession of the land. It was apparent that by some social upheaval they had been taught to depend on some one beside themselves, until individuality and manhood, had both alike departed.

I now saw in my dream that the sun was going down over the mountains in the distant west, while the shadows of night were gently falling. and it behooved me to seek shelter before the darkness should make it impossible to do so. In my flight I drew near to a mountain, on the far sloping sides of which there waved a vast forest of evergreens, which in the last beams of the setting sun made it seem like one great emerald set over against the golden sunset sky. Through a chance opening in the arms of the forest, I passed into its kindly shelter and easily alighted. It was already quite dark within those shades, and I hastened along a well beaten path, which leading up from the vale below, promised to bring me to a human habitation.

At a short turn in this path, I suddenly found myself in front of a massive stone edifice, plainly though somewhat quaintly built; surrounded by a small plot of ground, well kept and artistically arranged. A broad walk led from the gate, which swung open at my near approach; up to the front of the house. The entrance was closed with a curiously carved old oaken door, at which, after a moment's hesitation, I knocked for admittance. A deep rich toned voice, though somewhat broken as of an aged person, said, "Come in." With some little exertion I opened the door and entered. At the farther side of the room, which was quite large, sat an old man in front of an old fashioned fire place, in which a fire was burning with peculiar colored lights and shades.

He arose as I entered, and looked at me with a marked degree of astonishment. This was certainly reciprocated on my part, for I could not remember ever having seen so remarkable a personage. He stood more than six feet tall, erect, well built, and on his broad shoulders a massive head covered with a luxuriant growth of hair white as wool, while his heavy, wavy white beard fell to his waist. His eye was bright and piercing, while everything about him betokened unusual physical and mental strength. Having removed my hat as I entered, I advanced toward him in a most apologetic manner, while saying: "Kind sir, I am brought to this place and set down at your door by whom, and for what purpose I cannot tell; but if you will be so kind as to give me shelter for the night, I will with early dawn depart, to find my way down to the valley below, and give you no farther trouble.

With a pleasant and yet most wondering air he moved toward me, and extending his hand said: "You are most cordially welcome, and such as we have we freely give. We call this the Palace Heartway, after one of our most celebrated social reformers of the last century, of whom you have doubtless heard; and no stranger has ever been turned from our door." "Perhaps," he said, "for one like you appear to be, the isolation of this place may have no charms, but to myself and aged wife it is a place of rest which the busy world in the valley below, cannot give. However, be seated," he said, "and when our frugal meal is ready you shall sup with us." Although the name of the place and the great reformer somewhat puzzled me, as I could not recall that I had heard them before; yet I expressed myself as best I could with being highly gratified with such a shelter, and in such a place, and seating myself at his bidding I endeavored to compose myself for conversation,

After a moment of silence the old man turned to me and said, "Stranger, from whence do you come, and to what people do you belong? for, although your language is understood, yet your accent, tone and dress, indicate that you are not a citizen of this country." I said, "I am an American citizen, and free born, but whether I am a citizen of *this* country, or no, I cannot tell; for I do not seem to know where I am, nor can I give any true account of what has brought me here; I only know I am here, and shall most thankfully accept your kind hospitality." Observing my evident embarassment at being questioned concerning myself, he politely desisted, and calling his wife from an adjoining room he attempted to introduce me, but said, "I must first know your name." I answered, "my name is R. E. Former," as I returned the old lady's salutation; while she as kindly as had her husband, extended welcome to their hospitality.

I began to feel an indescribable awe in the presence of these august personages, for the wife was equal in intellectual force, and physical perfection, to her husband. The snows of an hundred winters seemed to have fallen upon them, and yet they both were vigorous in muscular action, and their eyes were undimmed. Their dignity of manner, and sweetness of intercourse, won my admiration and at the same time it gave me such a sense of inferiority that it was painful. I was soon again seated near the fire, and again noticed its peculiarity; for while it burned with vigor, and gave out plentiful heat, that which looked to me like wood remained unconsumed. I thought this is some new art, some new discovery with which my people were unacquainted. I could not bring myself to ask for information and so dismissed the matter from my mind.

My aged friend soon arose and excusing himself

for awhile, that he might attend to such arrangements as were necessary for the night, passed out of the room followed by his noble lady, and I was left alone. I felt sadly bewildered and confused. All about me was so strange and at times would take on such fantastic shapes and whirl before my eyes with immense velocity. By a desperate effort, however, I rallied, and began a closer inspection of the room. The furniture was all unique in pattern and finish. It looked heavy and firm but felt light and unsubstantial. The pictures on the walls were strange, both in design and execution. The portraits were of men I had never known, and the little ornaments about the room were all of strange material. At one side of the room stood a large book case extending along nearly its whole side and rising from floor to ceiling. This case was filled with volumes great and small; papers, magazines, pamphlets, and manuscript. Desirous of forgetting for awhile the strangeness of my surroundings I walked to the case, opened it, and began the examination of the books which it contained. My first observation was that most of the volumes were in appearance exceedingly old, while at the same time the dates of most of them were recent. In fact many of them were so worn and defaced as in many places to be scarcely legible; and yet the names of their authors were perfectly familiar to me, as were also the subjects of which they treated.

There was one book which especially attracted my attention. It was leather bound and bore the date of 1887; yet by its appearance one could scarcely believe that its leaves had been turned for a century.

It was entitled "Looking Backward," and seemed to be a sort of romance on social problems. Over this and many others of its class for a long time I pored with great interest. Not far removed from these, I saw a number of new works in appearance, and I eagerly scanned their titles. They all seemed to me, to treat on very strange subjects. Among them were, "The Decline and Fall of the old Republic," "History of the Social Revolution," "The Impending Disaster of the Military Republic," "The Decline of Literature," "History of the Overthrow of the Christian Sabbath," "Causes of the Decrease in Population," "The Destruction of American Industries," &c. These and many others which I cannot now recall were there. But the strangest, most bewildering fact of all was that these bore dates ranging from 2050 to 2090. I rubbed my eyes and looked again and again. Certainly I thought this must be a typographical error. But how could it appear in them all? Why were these new and the others old?

My bewilderment momentarily increased, until suddenly, having thrown myself into a large arm chair which stood near, I fell into one of those peculiar phantasmas with which one is often afflicted in dreams, and thought I saw a large enclosure into which there came running from all directions the literary celebrities of many ages. They were all solemnly or grotesquely arrayed to represent the character of their literary productions. Some looked wise, and some otherwise. They were old and young, rich and poor, male and female. Some crawled on the ground like serpents, while others seemed to pass along without touching the earth. Some had wings and the wings of some had been clipt. My attention was especially called to a number who pranced around on stilts, or hobbled on crutches, disdaining all their cotemporaries.

One whose name I learned was Bell Amy, came rushing along on remarkably high stilts, stepping over the throng about him. I saw written on the side of one of these game legs these words: "All virtues are developed and all vices destroyed, by simply assuring mankind of the full gratification of their natural wants." On the other it said, "A community of goods, under the paternal care of the government, is the ultimate of national destiny, and the acme of human happiness." But the most comical part of his appearance arose from the fact that he had been born a kind of logical monstrosity, his face being on the wrong side of his body, he was always looking backward; making progress only in the direction which he could not see.

There was also another remarkable personage, who went on crutches that had been cast away by some cripple in a former age. He had many followers whose only blasphemous utterance, when excited, was, "By George." It was remarkable with what entire unanimity they used this oath. One of the crutches on which he limped was called "single tax," and the other "Free Trade." He was busy abolishing poverty, and judging from the appearance of the money bag which he carried, he had succeeded in his own case admirably. The entrance of the old man called me back from my phantom chase, and hastily restoring the volumes to their places, I readily complied with his polite request to step out to tea.

---

## CHAPTER II.

Being seated at the table I found the repast to consist of several articles of plain food, well prepared, to which I was helped without apology. Before partaking of it, however, my venerable friend in simple language returned thanks to God the giver. Our conversation soon turned on the peculiarities of our meeting together, and although I was not able to give any satisfactory account of myself the good couple did not refuse to satisfy my curiosity concerning themselves. In reply to my question concerning the time which they had spent in that retired spot, they assured me that I had arrived on the seventy-fifth anniversary of their wedding day, and that all their married life with the exception of some years spent in travel, had been passed there. A large family of children had been reared there, who had now gone out into the world; some of them having entered into rest. They spoke with pride of their standing and character and of the honors which had been conferred upon them by their fellow citizens. The mother said it seemed very lonesome sometimes, and that she longed to hear again the laugh of childhood, and the music of prattling tongues resounding through the sil nt rooms. The tears stole down her cheek as she spoke of one, the youngest, the dearest, her pride, a beautiful daughter who, lured from home by the specious promises of one who addicted to the use of strong drink was unworthy the hand of any woman, and from whom she returned, broken hearted, to die in her mother's arms.

Mr. Right Pathfinder, for such I learned his name to be, assured me that although a laboring man from his youth yet he had found time to study carefully the great social questions of his own and previous ages. That having lived for so many years in the midst of the greatest social revolutions ever known among men, he had had a remarkable opportunity to study these matters by actual observation, as well as by a thorough acquaintance with all the history of the past. In all these investigations his amiable wife had been his constant associate and helpmeet, and was not one whit behind her husband in the keenness of her research, nor the solidity of her conclusions. She was at once wife, mother, scholar, philosopher, politician and Christian. They gave me to understand that they had not retired to this place as a hermitage, but were in daily communication with their neighbors in the vale below, and especially in the great city of Bellamy which lay only a few miles distant, where they had many acquaintances and friends. They casually remarked that they went to this place in order to draw their rations from the government. I did not quite understand this statement but asked no questions.

These facts seemed to please me greatly for I felt that I had at last met with some one who could instruct me along lines which I very much wished to investigate. But as the conversation proceeded I found myself profoundly puzzled by their allusions to matters of recent date, and to historical facts of great importance of which I had no knowledge. My host noticed this and rallied me on my perfect acquaintance with matters of two centuries gone by, while my memory seemed to fail me in all things of a late date. He finally incidentally mentioned that the then present day of the month and year was January 1st, 2101, and that it had closed one of the most remarkable centuries in human history.

I started with surprise so undisguised that both my friends took notice of it. My readers will doubtless sympathize with me in the perplexities of my situation. I began inwardly to inquire, "am I in the body or out of the body? Hath a spirit flesh and bones as I feel I have? Have I gone daft, has a sudden madness seized me?" Here I sat more than two hundred years ahead of myself, under a hospitable roof and at a well ordered board, not able to tell my entertainers whence I came, where I journied, nor what was the nature of my errand. All this I again confessed to my friends and begged their indulgence and forbearance, until I could in some measure regain myself. The repast was finished almost in silence when we arose and returned to the room which I had first entered. My venerable friend walked to the library and took down a well worn volume and before seating himself he said, "our habit has ever been to read from this book and commend ourselves to God before retiring for the night; if you wish to join us you are welcome to do so." I signified most earnestly my desire to remain with them which seemed to give my friends great satisfaction. The old man opened the book and read:

"Lay not up for yourselves treasures upon earth, where moth and rust doth corrupt and where thieves break through and steal.

"But lay up for yourselves treasures in heaven, where neither moth nor rust doth corrupt and where thieves do not break through nor steal.

"For where your treasure is there will your heart be also.

"The light of the body is the eye: If therefore thine eye be single, thy whole body shall be full of light.

"But if thine eye be evil thy whole body shall be full of darkness. If therefore the light that is in thee be darkness, how great is that darkness?

"No man can serve two masters; for either he will hate the one and love the other; or else he will hold to the one, and despise the other. Ye cannot serve God and mammon.

"Therefore I say unto you, take no thought for your life, what ye shall eat, or what ye shall drink; nor yet for your body, what ye shall put on. Is not the life more than meat, and the body than raiment.

"Behold the fowls of the air: for they sow not neither do they reap nor gather into barns; yet your heavenly Father feedeth them. Are ye not much better than they?

"Which of you by taking thought can **add one cubit unto his stature?**

"And why take ye thought for raiment? **Consider**

the lilies of the field how they grow; they toil not, neither do they spin:

"And yet I say unto you, that even Solomon in all his glory was not arrayed like one of these.

"Wherefore if God so clothe the grass of the field, which to-day is, and to-morrow is cast into the oven, shall He not much more clothe you, O ye of little faith?

"Therefore take no thought, saying, what shall we eat? or, what shall we drink? or, wherewithal shall we be clothed?

"(For after all these things do the Gentiles seek:) for your heavenly Father knoweth that ye have need of all these things.

"But seek ye first the kingdom of God, and His righteousness; and all these things shall be added unto you.

How richly laden with peace and comfort was every thought of this lesson to my bewildered and inquiring mind. Here was something not new nor strange. For more than twenty centuries these words of the most profound philosopher our world ever knew, had brought wisdom and comfort to burdened hearts and had proven themselves the key with which to unlock the store house God keeps well filled for his children's daily need. The selfish, darkened heart might not understand their lofty import, but to the believing soul it was sweeter than honey and the honeycomb.

The reading concluded the old people sang in sweet tremulous tones, and with an unction to me before unknown the following lines:

"Deem not that they are blest alone
"Whose days a peaceful tenor keep;
"The Anointed Son of God makes known
"A Blessing for the eyes that weep."

"The light of smiles shall fill again
"The lids that overflow with tears;
"And weary hours of woe and pain
"Are promises of happier years."

"There is a day of sunny rest
"For every dark and troubled night;
"And grief may bide an evening guest
"But joy will come with early light."

"Nor let the good man's trust depart,
"Though life its common gifts deny,
"Though with a pierced and broken heart,
"And spurned of men he goes to die."

"For God has marked each sorrowing day,
"And numbered every secret tear;
"And heaven's long age of bliss shall pay
"For all his children suffer here."

If the word was food, the song was drink to my thirsty soul. When ended my host knelt down and into the ever open ear of the Allmerciful, Allbountiful, Heavenly Father, he breathed in earnest accents his heartfelt petition. His first sentences were filled with praise and thanksgiving for the mercies of the day and then for those who had gone forth from the parental roof he prayed that they might be protected. For his neighbors and friends, for the sick and afflicted. And then for his country in its lost and ruined condition; for the worldly selfish and polluted church; for the restoration of the Lord's day, and for the salvation of the people from revelling, drunkenness, licentiousness and unbelief. For me, the stranger, he petitioned the throne that God would guide and help me. To all this prayer, though some of its allusions I could not understand, I responded down deep in my heart, Amen.

Soon after the devotions were ended the good wife excused herself and I was left alone with the husband. He invited me to an easy seat near a table, on which some books were laid, he occupying a place on the other side. I was much pleased to observe that those twin vices represented by wine and cigars were not to be cultivated during our conversation as we needed not the volubility of the one, nor the stupefying brutality of the other, to aid us in the discussion of reformatory questions.

I ventured to open the conversation by saying, "You will pardon me Mr. Pathfinder if I ask you to do me the favor of making a full statement of our surroundings, together with the history of this strange place, and of the people which I saw to-day as I came to this mountain, and to your hospitality. It seems to me that your hour of worship has so soothed my bewildered mind that I can bear now to hear whatever you may have to say." To this he replied, "I will most gladly comply with your request; but first, cannot you now give me some account of yourself and of your mission hither, that I may speak of that which would most interest you." I replied, "I will try and do so although I am not yet clear in my own mind as to how I came to be in this place. But of some matters which have been uppermost in my mind for some time past I think I can speak freely, and concerning these matters I would like to inquire. I am a citizen of the United States of America, and to me this is the year of Our Lord 1890. As I said this the old man looked at me with such intense surprise that it tried me severely; but mastering myself I proceeded to say: "I am an earnest seeker after truth, and have been giving especial attention to the great social problems which so deeply affect my race and nation. The age in which I live is remarkable for its social unrest, and for its determined efforts for the betterment of the great laboring classes, and for freedom for body and soul. So keenly alive are the intelligent masses to the situation, that they are constantly in danger of being duped by pretended reformers, many of whom have never associated with them, and know nothing by actual experience of their needs. There are many usages and laws of my time which tend unrighteously to make the rich richer, and the poor, poorer. Wealth rolls in splendor, while poverty drags itself onward in wretchedness and sorrow. Crime is rampant, politics are viscious. Bribery in elections is common and large minorities of the leading classes love to have it so.

It is but just, however, to say, that the virtue, honor, integrity and charitableness of vast numbers of my people excel that of any age of the world. It costs a man more to be mean now than ever before in human history. So true is this that hundreds commit suicide rather than endure the scorn of their fellow men. The courts yet rise above the vice, and pollution about them, and for the most part judge righteously as between man and man. By far the majority of the Christian ministry are true to themselves, their calling, and their God. Brave men and women everywhere are making a desperate fight against the corrupting influences which are spreading in both church and state. Great disasters by sea and land, at home and abroad, involving the loss of life and property, have occurred of late, and have tested the kinship in suffering, of our people. To these demands they have responded nobly, pouring out goods and money like water for the alleviation of human suffering.

What we seem to need most is that society shall be so ordered, and government so administered, as to give men and women a fair and equal chance to work out their own destiny, to meet and overcome the necessary antagonistic forces of matter and mind, with which the all-wise Creator has surrounded them. The personal freedom of the citizen in our country has greatly intensified his individualism. Liberty, by an eternal law of nature involves antagonisms. The tyranny of a centralized government breaks down both freedom and manhood. For myself I must say that I believe that all history teaches that the only successful co-operation of men in society, must be one voluntarily entered into by each individual for himself. The most remarkable illustration of the absurdity of national socialism, is that of the building of the tower of Babel, which God overthrew by the confusion of tongues. Pure individualism is freedom at its best; honest co-operation then becomes possible. What to do in order to preserve the good we have, and to prevent the disasters which threaten my people is the burden of my heart. And now, kind sir, if you can aid me in this, and I am permitted to return to my people, I promise you to do all in my power to instruct them in the way of righteousness and security.

During all this long speech the old man had watched me with intense curiosity. He hesitated a moment and then said, "you have given me no easy task, and I am much surprised at the accuracy of your statement concerning the needs of the age of which you speak. Permit me to assure you that this is indeed more than two hundred years later in earth's history than the time you name, and I am still at a great loss to understand you, as well as how I am to make you understand me. However, he said very kindly, I will not increase your bewilderment, but will do what I may to assist you in your lawful pursuit of knowledge, concerning the important subjects which you name. It is most certainly your own country over which you passed to-day, but if history has not deceived us it is in a woeful plight in comparison with the favored age in which you lived. His words, "you lived" so shocked me that for some moments I felt a faintness creeping over my whole body, and strange fancies siezed my brain. I thought then surely I must have been dead two hundred years. Where have I been? How is it that within these few hours I have awoke to consciousness? Is this Hades of which I have heard the theologians debate? My friends, where are they, and my countrymen, the busy toilers whose cause I loved, what has been done for them. If perchance I could learn anything which would bring them relief could I return and deliver my message, and would they believe if one should thus "arise from the dead." A soft hand placed on my brow recalled me to consciousness, and I opened my eyes to see my venerable friend leaning over me with great anxiety depicted in his face.

I said I am all right now, thank you. It was only the recurrence of a phantasy with which I am frequently seized, and I beg you hereafter to give yourself no uneasiness about me. When seated I asked him to proceed with his explanation. Cautiously he resumed: "I have given much attention to the history of the latter half of the nineteenth century, and must say that the movements began then, have played a most important part in the destiny of our nation. Seeds were sown then which in one hundred years ripened into a terrible harvest, the full fruitage of which the century just past has garnered in pain and tears. We name the nineteenth the "Golden century" of the ages. I have here in my library the works of all the celebrated authors of that day, and have made a careful study of their schemes of political economy, for more than half a century. During this time we have had the results of their efforts on trial and they have formed an object lesson of superior interest. I have passed over our country from Alaska to Yucatan, (this struck me as a new item in the geography of the country) and in the light of what their experiments have cost I must say that they have proven the greatest social and moral failure which history records. I shall not leave you to rely solely on my word for these facts, but if you remain with us for a brief period I shall be only too happy to accompany you into the surrounding country, that you may see for yourself the dire results of their policy.

But I must not weary you with a farther conversation on these matters to-night; but on the morrow will gratify you to the extent of my ability. Permit me to show you to the guest chamber, and to wish you a cheerful good night. Saying this he arose, and without a word of protest I followed him. He led the way to an adjoining room which was large and airy, and quite plainly yet comfortably furnished. I passed in and closed the door while saying a single good night. I threw myself on the couch and made one more desperate effort to account for myself, to myself; but it was all in vain. I fell on my knees and prayed to Him who changes not, to have mercy on my bewildered soul. The answer came and a sweet peace filled all my being as I lay down to rest.

When Morpheus had but just claimed me for his own I fell into one of those dreadful phantasmas and thought I saw a long line of very literary looking personages, who were said to be social reformers, standing in an open court, evidently preparing to play a game of leap frog. Each bent low behind his fellow, and grasping firmly his boot straps made desperate attempts to leap. They tugged and pulled, and shouted angrily, and cursed the law of gravitation which would not let them rise, until finally I saw that through their desperate efforts their shoulder blades were being displaced and rising up, and pushing forward, until they seemed to form an attachment at the sides of their heads; when suddenly there was a change in the scene and I found myself peering through a fence at a herd of donkeys, that some drover had corralled for the night.

## CHAPTER III.

The morning came and with it I awoke, to be made aware that a dismal storm was raging without. I could hear the down pouring of the rain, the soughing of the wind through the great pines on the mountain side. I lay reflecting for a time on my singular surroundings, then hastily arising I committed myself in prayer to my kind Heavenly Father, and then passed out into the family sitting room where I was pleasantly greeted by the old gentleman and his wife who had preceeded me. Again the old book was taken down and read and I was politely asked to lead in the devotions. With a strange commingling of hope and fear, faith and doubt, I tried to speak to my best friend, my compassionate Heavenly Father. I remember that I prayed for myself, my hospitable friends and my dear wife and children. I did not forget to make supplication for those in authority, for President Harrison, and his cabinet, and for the congress of the United States then in session.

I observed immediately as I arose from my knees that I was regarded by my friends with increased curiosity. To pray for a president who had been dead for nearly two hundred years, and for a cabinet and congress whose names and fame had long since been forgotten was enough to surprise anyone. But what else could I do? What else did I know? For what else could I feel a want which might be expressed in prayer? I felt myself the incongruity of the whole matter, but this served only to increase the density of the cloud which seemed to hang over my whole being. My host however soon led the way to the breakfast table. I took the opportunity to more carefully inspect the furnishing of the dining room and of the kitchen beyond, the door of which had been left open. There was no sign of a fire anywhere and yet although the weather was cold and chilly without, the room was warm and the food had been properly prepared. The table ware had a peculiar lightness about it for which I could not account and although beautifully inlaid and overlaid to represent metal or china ware, yet I was assured that they were made of paper and would neither break nor wear out in a life time. The good lady proudly showed me a set which constituted a part of her wedding presents, every piece being perfect.

Breakfast over we retired again to the room which I felt somehow was to be the school room where I was to be taught that which most of all I desired to know, how shall the great masses of mankind be liberated from the thraldom of vice, penury, and sin; and given a fair chance to develope their God-given powers. The storm without still raged and I felt a pleasure in the thought that now nothing would be likely to disturb our conversation; it was that sense of security which one feels when **shut in** from the world, even by a storm. I was made to feel somehow when we were seated that the old man wished me to lead in the conversation, lest he should introduce something which might needlessly distress me. I therefore ventured to ask him if really the United States at the date which he claimed the present to be was still in existence, and if he would favor me with some of its history. That while I could not realize that any such time had elapsed since I had taken an active part as one of its citizens, yet nevertheless, I desired him to speak freely and fully what he must know concerning this matter.

To this he readily assented. In reply to your question, he said, I must inform you, sad as the fact may be to you, that the United States is a nation of the past, both in its boundaries and form of government. The people about us are the descendants of those with whom you associated and this great country is the same. But he continued no one can justly describe the terrible sufferings through which they have come, and their fathers have endured before them, neither he said can one well describe the low condition to which the whole country has fallen.

In the latter part of the twentieth century, about nineteen hundred and seventy-five, the great social upheaval which had been long delayed, broke forth with intense fury. The restless masses, goaded on by foreign renegades, and duped by those who led them by false methods to attempt the settlement of great social questions, and becoming blind to all things else but their own real and fancied wrongs, they inaugurated a campaign of destruction to life and property unequaled in the annals of history. Like as in France years ago the red blood of the slain ran in the streets, so again was there a reign of terror. The country was not divided section against section, but it was a hand to hand conflict under local leaders; flaunting the red ffag of anarchy and socialism.

During this announcement of my beloved country's downfall, I had become so excited as to arise to my feet and leaning toward my informer, I listened with every fibre of my being drawn to its greatest tension. Observing my evident distress he paused a moment, and when I was reseated cautiously resumed by saying, perhaps you could bear this matter better if I were to give you in advance some of the causes which led to these awful results. Having partially composed myself I urged him to proceed in the manner he deemed best. From a careful study of the history of the nineteenth century, and the early part of the twentieth, with whose historians I am cotemporary, said he, I think I may be able to point out some at least of the rocks on which the government and the social fabric of the United States stranded.

The first great mistake of the nation, and that which increased constantly as it advanced in years, was the attempt to assimilate antagonistic elements into the American social system. Lured by its broad acres, enticed by its liberal laws, hundreds of thousands of men and women totally unfitted by habit and education to become citizens of that free government, were received, given homes and enfranchised, ere they knew the first principles of a republic. As I looked over the names of the leaders of mobs, riots and rebellions, I observed that very few of them were American born. These leaders were born under tyranny, and nurtured in hot beds of infidelity and liberalism, disregarding alike the laws of God and man. They came to that people to instruct them in liberty, and to lead them from the bondage of law and order, to the chaos of anarchism and crime. So long as society held with some degree of tenacity to the civilization of Plymouth Rock, with its sturdy observance of law, both human and divine, the assimilating process was possible; but with a departure from this, accompanied by derision of Puritanism, and a declaration of liberty for all human propensities, then came the beginning of the end of the process.

As an outgrowth of this slackening of moral obligation, there grew up an almost utter disregard for the civil and religious Sabbath, as the fathers had observed it. The church in itself became slack in its religious observance of the Lord's day, and the civil Sabbath was either disregarded entirely or used as a holiday for all manner of good and wicked diversions. The government as well as great corporations violated the Sunday rest law with impunity. Millions who ceased from labor on that day gathered in the public places of resort. Saloons and gambling houses were kept open and thus this mass of idlers increased and became more demoralized, until the day became a social curse instead of a blessing. From the higher standpoint of moral obligation such a desecration of God's holy day could but bring disaster to the nation.

Secretism also made rapid and dangerous progress. While some secret societies were organized and conducted for good ends, the system itself was vicious. What was originated for personal protection was conducted for the overthrow of the rights of others. Caste was established, the people were divided along unnatural lines, cutting society up into cliques and laying the foundation for unnecessary antagonisms among men. An almost irresistible temptation was by these oaths of brotherhood brought to bear upon office holders, having appointing power, upon judges, juries, and in all commercial transactions to unrighteously discriminate between men, and to thwart the ends of justice in dealing with criminals. Taking their cue from these comparatively harmless organizations, the enemies of the government and the social system, bound together by horrid oaths, plotted in secret their schemes of death and destruction, and from the lodge room went forth to execute them. Some of these orders became in time the very hotbeds of treason, and furnished the mobs with leaders of the most criminal character. When the final disaster came they played a very important part in the overthrow of the nation.

But the most direct agency in the ruin of the great republic was the alcoholic liquor traffic. Among social horrors it was king. No system of corporate robbery, no combination of trusts, in any manner approached this traffic which worse than wasted the resources of the nation. It snatched the bread from the hungry and fired its victim with madness against the innocent. The business violated every law enacted for its control, and was essentially a traitor to God and man. Its waste of the nation's resources was simply enormous. I observe by consulting some of the most reliable statistics of that day that the loss of time and industry reached the aggregate of $600,000,000. The loss by the amount spent directly for liquors, $750,000,000; to this must be added the value of 40,000,000 bushels of grain destroyed for drink, $30,000,000; and then again increased taxation reached not less than $100,000,000; making a total of annual loss of $1,480,000,000; to this add the waste by the tobacco habit, $600,000,000; grand total, $2,080,000.

The people called for bread, shouted themselves hoarse against the monopolies which deprived them of it, and then spent enough for liquors and tobacco to have clothed and fed the whole population comfortably. And remarked Mr. Pathfinder with great earnestness, I look in vain in the works of these social reformers who flourished in your time to find any attempt to stop this leak. Their socialist leaders set down to discuss social problems over wine and cigars; while the orators who inflamed the populace, were themselves inflamed with wine. This fact marks the utter selfishness of these reformers and their entire want of moral principle. They wept over the sorrows of the struggling, poverty stricken masses, and yet never lifted a hand to turn back this stream of death, because forsooth; it was upopular to oppose this crime of crimes.

Alcoholic liquors vitiated the blood of the nation; ruined families, divorced husbands and wives, wrought arson, theft, burglary, gambling, licentiousness, and murder. Disobeyed law, and then made the breach of the law an argument for its repeal. The saloon became the headquarters of anarchism and from its doors the red flag representing destruction to all government was flaunted. By sapping the physical and moral strength of the individual citizen they sapped the very foundations of the republic. Our historinas say, that when the fearful struggle for the nation's life came on, th s business which had spared neither young nor old in peace became in war a devil incarnate. It demoralized officials, made drunken officers, and maddened with its fiery potations the suffering masses.

And my dear sir, will you if possible explain why as our histories of those times inform us, the authorities well knowing the nature of this awful crime continued to foster and protect it. I have been told that under the old republic the government actually took a share of the profits arising from the conducting of this business and sold the right to continue it, from year to year; although it invariably broke the license contract. Some were even foolish enough to suppose that they could eradicate such an evil, while selling it the right to exist. That the great license system, as it was called, although from the beginning a fraud, and a failure, was continued as a governmental policy long after the treasonable nature of the business was known to every citizen. While our own **times** are crimsoned with the gore of the millions slain by this vice, yet the system of bribes which sustained it in those days has been abolished.

The power of the liquor traffic in politics gradually increased, the public conscience was more and more hardened by it. If a single citizen was made to suffer by a foreign foe, then the nation would be stirred with resentment; but when the same citizen was robbed, debauched or slain by this internal enemy, no voice in authority was raised against the wrong. No great social reformer advocated the abrogation of the liquor traffic; this was left to men who dared to be martyrs to the cause of right. Many such were organized into a political party and were sustained by a band of noble women, but the conscience of state and church were seared and all efforts were unavailing The masses went with the selfish leaders who espoused their cause and did not rebuke their vices.

The day was now far spent. To me it had been wonderfully full of interest, while we discussed the foregoing and kindred subjects. The after tea conversation was joined in by the good lady of the house and was mainly of a social character. I found her a woman of decided opinions well matured. She spoke feelingly of the bright hopes which filled so large a place in the hearts of her ancestors, that with the new order of things there would come an emancipation of her sex, from the unnatural and enforced disabilities, under which, through unjust and unequal legislation they had always suffered. But those hopes were all to be blasted at the last by the utter selfishness of masculine social leaders, who saw nothing of virtue but as a product; of well filled stomachs and well dressed bodies.

On retiring that night I had no sooner fallen asleep, than I saw in my dreams an immense body of water, known as Working Man's Pond. In this were kept a large number of fish, which were of great value to their owners. This pond was supplied by a number of small rivers and creeks, which emptied into it from the surrounding country. It seemed to me in my dream, that at times it was very difficult to keep this pond filled with water, and sometimes it looked as though all the fish must perish- At times these streams which fed the pond would be dammed up by certain great corporations, for their own selfish ends. They would thus shut off the flow of water, in order to raise ponds of their own, for the sake of power. By some syndicates these streams were diverted from their natural courses by sluice ways, and canals, leading into Trust River, and Bondholders Bay. At such times I saw numbers of men who seemed to have great interest in the fish, going up and down these streams, in order to discover some way to save the fish by increasing the supply of water.

I noticed one who rode in great haste up Wages river, and shouted to the inhabitants as he passed to unstop their fountains, and decrease as far as possible their use of water from the river. in order to increase its flow. Another went on a similar mission up Rent creek, demanding the confiscation of all the ponds and lakes which had been accumulated about the head of the stream. Monopoly river, also, was so unequal in its flow and so filthy and corrupt, that it distressed the fish and their owners greatly. A number of gentlemen in a very excited manner declared their intention to cut a passage through Moneyloaners Pass to Interest Bayou, and drain it dry. While all this was going on I took occasion to go down below the dam which had been made across the stream in order to raise the pond, and there I saw the water rushing out in torrents from certain large fissures known as Rum-holes.

I at once called the attention of these great philanthropists who were so much concerned about the fish to this fact, and said, "Why not stop the leaks? Close up these holes and stop this enormous waste." But they only shook their heads and "looking backward" with longing, up these various streams, said: "Your plan is impracticable. It can't be done. And if it could, it would be an unjustifiable interference with the rights of the Mullets, Bullheads, and Suckers, which infest the stream below." "And besides the animals which have opened these holes, have certain vested rights in them which we are bound to respect." So the waste went on, the holes enlarged, and the fish suffered and died.

As I stood looking in sadness over this field of desolation and death, suddenly the scene changed, and I thought I stood beside a great iron cage which contained a large number of poisonous reptiles. I saw that although they were apparently restricted by the bars of the cage, yet in fact there were holes left at convenient distances, out of which the serpents freely passed. And as I looked I saw that the people in great numbers were being bitten and many were already in the agonies of death. I saw that there were men standing at each of these holes in the cage who had the management of the work of the snakes. They seemed to be the enemies of all mankind and to delight in the destruction wrought by the serpents. In my zeal I ventured to remonstrate with them; but they tossed their heads and said, "We have the government's permission to open the holes, paying one hundred dollars a year for the privilege." "You mind your business and we will ours. If you feel so concerned about the sufferings of these poisoned ones, why do you not join the ranks of those who spend their years in sucking out the poison from the wounds which our serpents have made."

But so destructive were these serpents and they did cause so much sorrow and pain, that there went up a bitter cry from all over the land. Then I saw in my dream a long procession of priests and preachers, elders and deacons, politicians and wholesale snake dealers, who went up with a long petition to the government praying them to make the license so high for these snake-holes that it would reduce them at least one half, and thus save the people. The government seemed to accede to this request, and the procession returned in triumph. As I turned to look at the cage behold half the holes were closed up, especially the small ones from whence the little snakes crawled out, but they finally all passed out through the holes left for the large ones, and lo! there was no decrease in the death rate caused by their poison. As I turned and looked upward I saw emblazoned on a passing cloud "What fools these mortals be."

## CHAPTER IV.

I was cordially welcomed the next morning at the breakfast table and finally in my "school room," where at my request the old gentleman continued his narration of the causes which conspired to overthrow the old republic. During all these recitals I seemed to be personally greatly pained, for of all these things which to my friend were matters of history I felt myself to be a part. He spoke of the church and the part which it took in the great social revolution. He spoke with great reverence for the church, as he was profoundly in love with its founder. To speak of her faults seemed to give him pain. He said, that the church more and more widely separated itself from the masses of the people. The vast sums of money expended in building churches excluded the poor from their pews. Gospel workers of various kinds seeing all this went out from the churches into the byways to save the people. But this by contrast only widened the breach. Hundreds of thousands of these abandoned ones were saved by these extraordinary appliances; but a vast majority of the members of the church were offended at the want of as thetic taste displayed by these street and hall workers and gave them little or no encouragement.

Great hearts both in pulpit and pew longed to break through these restraints and go to the people with the saving, civilizing, uplifting power of the gospel of the lowly Nazarene; but they were not able to escape the bondage of caste, habit and form. The founder of this church had declared the glory of the kingdom to be that the "poor have the gospel preached unto them;" but when rich men became a necessity to the church because of its "manner of living," then the glory of the gospel was that the rich and fashionable people hear the gospel regularly. The question was, shall the rich go down to the poor or shall they sit in their luxurious rented pews and wait for the poor to come to them. Everywhere there were men and women who in a small way sought to and did overcome this barrier, and they were the "salt of the earth." Had not the mass of corrupting influences been greater than they could cover, they would have saved the nation. When the final crash came these remained true to God and the right, but the majority of the church having lost its savor "was cast out and trodden under the feet of men."

The appliances for the promulgation of the Gospel seemed to have been wonderfully developed, The church kept pace with the world in utilizing the great discoveries of that age in its work, but the difficulty was that in too many instances the "Living Spirit was not in the wheels." God had said, "It is not by might nor by power but by my spirit." Into some churches games of chance and various forms of gambling were introduced; foolish and misleading amusements also, until the church of the Holy Nazarene was made a hissing and a reproach, "My Father's house is a house of prayer but ye have made it a den of thieves."

Another difficulty which arose in the very nature of the case was, that the Christian workmen yielding a ready obedience to law, separating themselves from the lazy, drunken, wasteful portion of their fellow laborers, refusing to join in strikes and riots, "being content with their wages;" were able to clothe and feed their families in a respectable manner. This naturally aroused the jealousy of these lower classes, and instead of imitating their virtues, they began to hate the church, and to deride its members as above their master. The fact of the whole matter was that God to this people had fulfilled his promise. "That the righteous should not be forsaken nor his seed be found begging bread." Yet thus the breach was widened between the people and the "Son of Man," even by the very good for which the uneasy classes clamored. These followers of Christ remembered how he said, "In the world ye shall have tribulation, but be of good cheer I have overcome the world," He did not promise the removal of the antagonisms but rather "My grace shall be sufficient for you."

The closing quarter of the nineteenth century seemed to develope to an abnormal degree, these, and kindred separating elements in society. The inventive genius of man was taxed to its utmost in the creation of destructive weaponry, as well as for those which might aid in the peaceful pursuits of manufactures and husbandry. The agriculturist had been supplied with such labor saving machinery that one man might do the work of ten, as performed in the old fashioned way. This greatly cheapened the price of all farm commodities, while by increased production it forced a wider market. This was true also of all manufactures where machinery took the place of skilled muscle. The use of machinery was not therefore necessarily disastrous to the interests of working men. The chief difficulty arose from the fact that these goods thus cheapened, and placed within the reach of the poorer classes, consumption was enormously increased, and the laboring people departing from the simplicity and frugality of their fathers, as in some measure it was their right and privilege to do; stopped not however at a reasonable gratification, but apeing the rich in their manner of living, racked body and soul to procure the means to maintain it.

This condition of affairs made money a necessity and the whole mass of the people plunged madly into the pursuit of wealth. Then the false antagonisms which led to the final ruin of the nation were born of selfishness and lust of gold. These antagonisms were largely artificial and resulted from too great a satisfaction of human wants. Large debts were incurred, both by individuals and corporations, including the government. The want of being obliged to cultivate economy on the part of so many, led, as it always will, to gormandizing, waste, and the destruction of conservative manhood. The rich degenerated in vital and mental forces, and the poor spent their days in longing for that which would have been their greatest curse.

During these years there was a large emigration from the old country, as it was called, not of their best blood but of the discontented and criminal classes —men who, under the iron heel of despotism, had learned to despise government and hate law. Whose only ideas of God, Christ and the church were founded upon their observation of the heartlessness of church formalism, mingled with the hellish machinations of designing priests, in the state churches of their native land. The degrading superstitions and debasing ignorance of the masses they largely credited to the church, which false to itself and to its Master, had established a system of church idolatry.

Many of those were professed anarchists and socialistic leaders, who recklessly stirred up the masses of the people who could be deceived by them, so that a universal uneasiness tending directly to riots, mobs, strikes and general defiance of law, was developed everywhere among the people. Communism born and baptised in the blood of the old French revolution made terrible inroads into the peace of society. Its doctrines were luring and deceptive. It offered a liberty which was simply license for unbridled passion. It deified the human and dethroned God from its conscience and life. It was Atheistic in all its tendencies, destructive in all its methods.

It had many phases of manifestation, and coming to the common people and lower classes while they chafed under the grinding power of monopolies and the heartlessness of corporations, its falsehoods found ready access to their heads and hearts, and developed rapidly into lawlessness and crime. Its devotees sought out the most destructive enginery and death-dealing missiles, and taught their children that it was right to use them. Their cry was, "Down with the government, down with the church, down with God." They taught that "the road to virtue lay through the gratification of man's natural desires." They clamored for the redistribution of wealth and said: "Make men free and you will make men holy." They published newspapers, tracts and books filled with fiery denunciations of the government, and on occasion did not hesitate to murder the officers of the law who attempted to restrain them. They organized bands of young people, which met in saloons or rooms adjacent, to be taught all their blasphemies, hatred of God and good men; and celebrated the anniversary of noted criminals who had been executed for high crimes against their fellow men. They marched through the streets of the great cities shouting "Bread or Blood," and yet by far the majority of them spent daily enough money for beer, whisky and tobacco to have furnished themselves and their families plentifully with bread. At the first these were nearly all persons of foreign birth, and many of them not citizens of the country. But as time wore on they were joined by many of the native born population which greatly increased their power and influence.

There were other forms of socialism beside this extreme wing of which I have been speaking, that held the same general principles, but were more judicious and wily in their advocacy. These gained a foothold among the better classes as the methods which they advocated were not so severe and reprehensible. The religion of Jesus of Nazareth had gained such an ascendency among the nations of the earth, that some of them endeavored to try to popularize their system by naming it "Christian Socialism;" at the same time rejecting the very fundamental doctrines of the christian system. There were among these, men and women of noble aspirations, who earnestly sought the good of mankind, whose hearts were better than their heads. They opposed what they termed the tendency of the age to extreme individualism, and proposed instead of the then present, a paternal form of government, with universal co-operation by law. Their extremists recognizing the legitimate trend of the whole movement declared for the destruction of all rights in private property, the confiscation of landed estates or their rentals, the abolition of money and interest, and a community of goods distributed by a central government to the people.

Their most elaborate scheme seemed to involve the organization of society into an industrial army; involving the seizure of all lands and personal property by the government, the proceeds of which were to be distributed equally per capita, while the supply was to be maintained by the labors of the people under overseers and taskmasters appointed by the government. All children were to be kept in school during their minority, and on becoming of age were to be enlisted into active army life for three years, at common labor, at the termination of which they were permitted to choose trades or avocations for themselves, in which they were to be instructed and thereafter continued in the employ of the government until they were forty-five years of age, when they were to be discharged with a life annuity.

While my aged friend had been going through with this recital, and although every fact was familiar to me, yet I became so absorbed and interested that I broke out with exclamations of delight, saying, what a wonderful scheme, what a Paradise restored. I said how happy a nation must be when it has settled all the great social and moral problems in this way. I shall not regret my transition over these centuries if it has brought me to such a civilization as this. My good friend said: You have certainly come to a civilization modeled after this Utopian dream, and I shall be able, by taking you over the country to show you its practical workings, and I doubt not your sorrow will be as great as the joy you now express, when you have completed your investigation. But before we go out to this work I must make you still more intelligent concerning the causes which brought about the great revolution, but as the day is far spent I deem it wise that we defer until the morrow our further conversation. After some hours spent in a social way I retired to rest my mind filled with curious inquiries concerning this new departure. This bringing mankind to a common level of labor and reward.

In my dreams that night I thought I came in my journey to a range of mountains, known as the "Mountains of Human Endeavor." Beyond them lay the wonderland of "Human Attainment." Along the sides of these mountains I saw paths and highways worn deep in the soil and rocks by the passing feet of the myriads who had preceded me. I saw in my dream the toiling millions then on the way; and observed the trials and difficulties which they had to encounter, some fainted and faltered on account of the steepness of the way, while others taking byways which promised to bring them with little or no effort to the summit soon were aroused to the fact that they had been deceived and were again at the base from whence they started. Some I saw were by favoring circumstances lifted up and carried on the heads of their fellows, but those who carried them could not with their burden rise, and traveled only in a perpetual circle.

There were some who sought to reach the summit by trampling under foot all who came in their way, but these were disappointed at last as their names and fame toppled and fell together. Among these thronging masses I saw here and there men and women who kept sturdily on their way. The opposition which they met was their strength, the antagonisms brought the possibility of victory. All they asked was freedom to do their best, the only absolute law they knew was the survival of the fittest. These were noble souls and as they passed upward they stooped to the right and to the left to help a struggling brother. Once at the summit they waved their palms of victory, and realized as they had not before that there is no excellence without labor, no victory without conflict, no coerced co-operation possible except by the dethronement of manhood, responsibility and freedom.

As I came near the base of the mountain determined to begin the ascent, I saw a number of distinguished looking individuals standing about a great machine across the end of which I saw written in large gilt letters the words, "National and Social Equalizer No. 1;" on one side I saw the words, "Universal Reducer;" and on the other, "Universal Inflator." While I stopped for a moment wondering what all this could mean one of the social philosophers who owned the machine approached me and voluntered to instruct me in its operation and design. He called my attention to something which I had not noticed before, that there was an opening made in the mountain of Human Endeavor, extending clear through to the valley of "Human Attainment" beyond. Into this he explained they had succeded in inserting a sort of pneumatic tube called "Socialism," and through it by the help of the machine which I saw, they projected their deciples into the valley of Attainment without trouble or difficulty on their part. In order that one might pass through without accident it was necessary that he should exactly fit the tube, and as all men were not built alike nor equal in size, they had invented this machine in order to prepare them for the passage.

But, I inquired, what will be the result in the case of the man when he gets beyond the mountain. Will he be of any good in the valley. Will the bones which you have broken rejoice? Perhaps not, he said, but then it will be better, easier and safer than to attempt to overcome the antagonisms of the mountain. All one has to do he said, is to surrender one's self entirely to the machine to be handled by it. It may crush ambition and destroy individualism, but on the other hand it will inflate mediocrity and put a premium on idiocy, as it is much easier and more delightful to be inflated than to be reduced. So sincerely and earnestly were these good points in the machine enunciated that I resolved to try the tube route myself, and observing at once my great need of inflation they put me in that side of the machine. The power was applied, my bones cracked, my skin distended, my eyeballs seemed starting from their sockets; when with a desperate attempt to free myself I sprang from the bed into the middle of the room and looking up I saw it was broad day-light.

## CHAPTER V.

When we were fairly seated for our daily talk my friend said, I think it best before narrating the history of the great revolution to give you to understand how the nation suffered from the abuse of the power of money in the hands of the few unscrupulous men and corporations, who squeezed the life blood from the laboring classes. First, in the purchase of labor. These Shylocks demanded their pound of flesh although it should uncover the very heart of the victim. Forgetting the perishable nature of labor as a commodity, they offered only the lowest market price, and by importation of foreign and degraded laborers made honorable competition in many places almost impossible. Many individuals and corporations in purchasing labor. totally ignored the fact that they were in honor bound to pay living wages, for work honorably performed.

In many places men were ground down under the heel of a despotism little better than chattel slavery. And women too toiling by day and night to eke out a scanty living for themselves and loved ones, felt the unpitying blast of selfishness pass over their lives, uprooting hope and sowing the seeds of despair and shame.

Second, in combinations without considering the rights of the laboring classes. Great trusts were formed in which only the welfare of the capitalists entering it were considered. Producers and consumers were systematically robbed. Small dealers were crushed and small producers were ruined. These great corporations and trusts served to point an illustration of the absurdities of enforced cooperation to which the nation had done well to have taken heed. In such organizations the few think, the many do the machine act. Manhood is turned to gall, and freedom is a phantom and a fraud.

In the third place, the power of money in procuring legislation adverse to the interests of the poor was notable. Politics were made vicious by it and only rich men were eligible to office, because only a long purse could win. All this stimulated the uneasiness of the masses and they were clamoring for the redistribution of wealth, and the overthrow of power.

Among the schemes proposed for the cure of these evils was one which more than all others served to precipitate the conflict, and make wide spread ruin and devastation in the republic. This was known as the confiscation of rent or Single Tax reform. These measures were rendered doubly dangerous on account of the character and standing of those who advocated them. The great leaders of this movement styled land-owners' "Capt. Kidds," demanded that the government should in justice seize and hold all land titles, and furnish lands for occupancy to the highest bidder for rent. Thus an open violation of vested rights by sacred compacts was advised in the name of honor, virtue and right. But hesitating they said, "This is right but it would cause a revolution." The truth of this statement the sequel will show-

To accomplish the end desired, however, they proposed to force the surrender or forfeiture of all lands, by the confiscation of their rental values, through the imposition of burdensome taxation. This they saw at once could not be done through the then present system of laying taxes, because sufficient increase on land could not be made if all goods and personal property must share. It became necessary for the carrying out of this scheme that a division both unnatural and unjust should be brought about in society, between landlords and the landless. The evils of landlordism, great as they were, were yet greatly overstated. The benefits of land to their owners were greatly overestimated. Land was placed in the same category with air, water, and sunshine; God's gifts which no man should monopolize.

The single tax was the entering wedge of this scheme. Few comparatively owned land, and the remainder would be glad to avoid. as they supposed, the payment of taxes. This they thought could be done by collecting all taxes from land owners, entirely ignoring the fact in political economy that all taxes are finally paid by the consumers, and that the single tax theory was simply one concerning who should advance their payment to the government, as it could not depend on following each article to the consumer, and then and there presenting its demand. Under the old regime the land owner advanced a portion, and placed the amount on the cost of the raw material. The manufacturer receiving the raw material, added the share collected of him to his productions and passed them into the hands of the wholesale dealer, and he to the retail dealer, each adding his share. The consumer paid this, as he did all other costs of bringing within his reach the supply for his daily wants.

Under the single land tax method the whole amount was to be massed and demanded of the producers. This was carried on down as in the other case, no man escaping who did any kind of business. Each found himself obliged not to advance his share with a continual widening of responsibility as the goods passed onward; but rather bearing the full burden of the whole. In the nature of the case this would not seriously affect the retailers, nor very disastrously the wholesalers, but on the comparatively few manufacturers and especially on the land holders, the farmers and agriculturists, it would fall with crushing power. Its design was to render the holding of large landed estates unprofitable, but it was in the nature of the case equally unprofitable to the smaller holdings.

This measure was carried into the politics of the country, and early in the twentieth century through the machinations of capitalists who had no interest in real estate; joined with the influence and ballots of the great masses of the landless, it finally prevailed and became a law of the land. The disasters wrought by it among the producing classes I will now attempt to describe. The first general effect produced by it was the legitimate outgrowth of the agitation. The laboring classes were taught to believe that in the ownership of land and its cultivation was to be found the highest possible moral and social attainment. It was to reform the vicious, make wise the simple, and banish crime. They were told that the system would deprive the lands of the rich of their speculative value, force their abandonment and open the way for them to occupy and appropriate for their own use. Thus long delayed justice was to be meted out to the "Capt. Kidds," and "Land-Pirates," who had so long oppressed them. They were therefore ready to seize the first opportunity of obtaining lands, removing to them, building homes, or entering those already built.

In order to make the law effective a very stringent act was necessary concerning the forfeiture of land titles, for the nonpayment of taxes; and for the eviction of their owners. Three years sufficed to work forfeiture, seize title, and reconvey the same to the highest bidder, including the payment of the accumulated taxes. Many thousands at once took advantage of these opportunities, thus removing from the open market as consumers great masses of people, and placing them at once among the producing class. This was done in face of the fact that over-production in the field of agriculture had brought farm productions down to ruinously low prices, and this sudden and immense addition to this form of industry brought widespread disaster. From this and such crop failures as arise from storms, drouth and insects, immense numbers were not able to advance their share of all the taxes necessary to support the government, and their eviction became a necessity.

In the meantime the rich landlords foreseeing the evil, had very largely sold their lands to the small farmers, and investing their monies beyond the reach of taxation, were far from being the punished criminals which the theory had intended. Year by year these taxes were added to forfeited buildings and as land values had been destroyed at any distance removed from actual use and occupancy, no one would take them from the hands of the state. Thus the government became greatly crippled in its finances, in fact bankrupt. Again it found itself involved in interminable lawsuits over defective tax titles, until the enforcement of the law became impossible.

But no less disastrous was it to the manufacturing interests. They had been promised exemption from all taxation on all personal property and improvements, but behold when they came to purchase the raw material for their use it came burdened with all the taxes for the support of the government, which they must advance or discontinue business. Thousands of them succumbed to this pressure and as the single tax had superceded all protective duties, the whole mass of American industries became involved in ruin, which was hastened by the competition of foreign producers. Under the reasonable, common-sense method of the wide distribution of the tax burden, enabling cheap production, these foreign producers at once took possession of the markets, adding another to the evils which were wrecking the whole system of American agriculture, together with cattle-raising and wool-growing.

Perhaps no greater delusion in political economy ever took possession of a civilized people than the single tax theory, as a method for the removal of the evils against which it was aimed. Matters grew rapidly worse. Eviction with all that hateful term means to a free people became common throughout the nation, and yet the government could not be sustained. It was observed that much of the difficulty of enforcement arose from the conflict of titles as between original owners, owners by tax title, and titles by mortgage foreclosure. The cases resulting occupied the larger portion of the time of the courts, and the matter seemed interminable.

The opportunity had now come for the original idea of the single tax theorists to be brought to the front, viz., that justice as well as expediency demanded that the State should seize all land titles, and lease the land to the highest bidder for rent. This should be done by right of eminent domain by the State, and this would simplify the whole matter and put a stop to these ruinous contests. The nation was in a fever of excitement—various forms of socialism were pressing for mastery. Anarchism was rapidly increasing Something must be done to relieve matters and that speedily. Unscrupulous men had come into power, in state and nation. The United States congress was little more than an organized mob. The state legislatures were no better, and state after state passed acts destroying private titles in lands and fixing the same in the government, which were then offered to the highest bidder for rent.

This action was based upon the following statement. Land is one of the gifts of nature which like air, sunshine and water should be free to all. They contended that there could be no honest personal title to land beyond the limit of actual occupancy, and that this should be based solely on the improvements made thereon. The prevalence of these opinions led to the action above described. This however at once precipitated the conflict, long delayed, but not unforseen, by some of the wiser and more conscientious statesmen of that age. The land owners refused to be sold out, and turned out for taxes. On the other hand the cry was down with the landlords. They have assumed proprietorship in God's gifts to men, and are but "Robber barons" and highwaymen.

The first shock felt, was of a commercial character; and was in the line of the destruction of all land values and their retirement from the market. With this came also the destruction of their utility as security for indebtedness. Churches, Colleges, Orphanages, Hospitals and all charitable institutions, found their rents confiscated, and their livings gone. Leases given for a term of years were nullified, and every owner found himself in competition with his neighbor, and his enemies; for his own home; his farm, the land occupied by him for any purpose. In bidding for occupancy by the payment of rent, the poorer classes suffered the most. Envy and malice held high carnival, as amid the wild scenes of the auction of firesides and homes, they hissed their bids that brought ruin to their victims.

In this dire emergency of the government, unable to enforce its demands, or protect innocent citizens, the bloody Anarchists saw their opportunity to strike. The great cities poured out their slime and corruption like streams of burning lava, devastating as they rolled onward. They began to take possession of the homes of the rich by mob violence, and meeting with resistance they resorted without compunction or pity, to their weapons of destruction. Dynamite bombs were hurled without remorse into magnificent structures scattering them to the winds and flames, The gas-mains of the cities were "doctored," and then exploded with terrible destruction, while conflagration after conflagration spread red ruin o'er the land. To stay these proceedings the government was powerless. The revolution predicted by the social leaders had come, and with it sin, shame, and despair.

The inefficiency of the general government led to open revolt on the part of the several states, who undertook their own protection. Into this general chaos was now hurled another element, long dreaded by your wisest statesmen. I refer to the immense colored population, whose ancestors had suffered the tortures of the hell of slavery. The cup of vengeance for a Christian civilization, that could tolerate for so many years such a crime against the image of God as American Slavery, was yet to be filled to overflowing. At the opening of the 20th century there were about twenty millions of these people in the country. Large numbers of them were yet debased by ignorance, benumbed by vice, and maddened by the unjust, and unrighteous proscription practiced upon them by the whites, who were formerly their masters; these now became under educated leaders, a most dangerous element in the contest.

They undertook the organization of a black republic, and being vigorously opposed by their white neighbors, a murderous, hand to hand, man to man, conflict ensued. In many portions of the country they were numerically greatly in the ascendency, and here their fiendish passions had full sway. The children of whites, whose grandfathers and great-grandfathers had sold colored babes by the pound, on the auction blocks of America; were dashed to death in sight of their parents, the mothers in many instances being humiliated to that which is worse than death. Among the most fiendish and brutal, were those in whose veins there flowed a portion of Anglo-Saxon blood, a legacy of the hellish crimes committed against the negro race when virtue in them was destroyed by law, and vice in their masters protected by legislative enactments. So curses like fowls, come home to roost; and the voice of blood crying from the ground is never stilled, until justice is meted out to offenders against humanity and God.

Intestine war now raged over all the land. It was a war of classes, of races. Brother against brother, father and son in deadly conflict. Great leaders were here and there developed who led their followers to battle with ever varying success. 'Many citizens, persecuted and in fear of their lives, fled to foreign countries and to Canada and Mexico. The shielding of these refugees by these goverments led to conflict with them, and within them, until the whole continent became involved in the struggle. Year after year passed by, gaunt famine and pestilence stalked abroad at midday. Gradually the better class of socialists came to the front with decided advantage; and after ten years of bloody strife, there was developed a great military genius euphonously named "Dick Tator", who extended his conquests over the whole continent, until utterly exhausted and subjugated it lay at his feet.

England had for a time taken a hand in the struggle in America to save her provinces, but the great uprising for a republic in Australia, an extensive war in Asia threatening her Indian possessions, together with a general war in Europe, and rebellion in Ireland, gave her sufficient work at home; and she finally relinquished all claim to any part of North America. Thus was the victory won which placed this whole continent under one government, obliterating both state and national lines.

The work of reconstruction now began in earnest. It was agreed that for the time, a strongly centralized government was demanded, one which might bring order out of chaos, and prepare the way for a constitutional form of government. It was said that the error of the nineteenth century republic was its intense individualism. This was to be avoided at all hazards. The whole plan must be communistic.

The ministers and convocations of the church of Jesus of Nazareth, had given great offense to these socialistic leaders; before, and at the beginning of the great revolution, in that they had denounced many of their theories and doctrines as purely Atheistic and dangerous. That they were selfish in the extreme, and having nothing but a secular basis, which entirely ignored the personality and providence of God, would invariably break and destroy the rights and liberties of the people. It was therefore determined that while tolerance should prevail in regard to religious opinions, yet the government sanction and support should be withheld, from anything distinctly religious.

Gen. Dick Tator was a man after their own heart, capable, self-reliant, patriotic. Not ambitious for power, a soldier in the best sense of the word; who thought there was no form of government so good as the military control of an army. He thoroughly believed in the possibility of a system of universal co-operation, and that the path to virtue, integrity and honor; lay along the line of the satisfaction of man's natural wants. From his brain was evolved the great system of a military republic. He prepared the way for a convention, which he called for the purpose of formulating a constitution, but was careful that the majority of them, should agree with him in his scheme for a military republic.

At this point in the conversation, I called my kind instructors attention to the fact that we had been several hours together, and that I could not think of taxing his generosity farther that day. After some hours in social recreation, and wandering about the garden and vicinity, I again laid down to rest under the protection of Him, "who giveth his beloved sleep."

## CHAPTER VI.

On the following day my host informed me that it was necessary for him to go to the city, to procure their weekly supplies, and as his good wife was to accompany him it might be rather a lonesome day for me at the Palace. He suggested that possibly I might be pleased rather to go with them. I thanked him kindly, but said that I should prefer spending the day in his library, as I felt that I had not yet sufficiently acquainted myself with my surroundings to make a visit out into society either agreeable or profitble. It was accordingly arranged that I should remain at home, and amuse myself as best I might for the day.

When their carriage disappeared through the pines, I turned from the window through which I had been watching it, and was soon seated at the library, determined to follow up the strange history to which I had been listening; as it came from the lips of my friend, in the books which he assured me contained the desired information. Taking down a book entitled, "The History of the Great Social Revolution," I began eagerly to scan its pages. The author had made an exceedingly compact compilation of facts,

## AND WHAT I SAW. 59

debates, State papers, and legal enactments, in order to show the animus, methods and outcome of the movement which had resulted in the present condition of things.

About the first thing to arrest my attention was a copy of the proclamation convening a constitutional convention as issued by Gen. Dick Tator a few months after the close of the war. It was brief, concise and manly, and bore evident marks of sincerity. It read as follows:

*To the People of North America Greeting:* I, Dick Tator, Commander in Chief of the Great United Army, and Provisional Governor General, do hereby issue and make known, this, my first general proclamation concerning the future welfare of this great nation. It is hereby ordered and directed, that a convention of our ablest and best men be assembled, for the purpose of formulating a constitution for a republic, and to enact such laws as shall be found necessary to bring such a constitution before the people for adoption. I do hereby appoint Tuesday, Nov. 2d, 1986, as the day for the holding of a general election for the purpose of choosing delegates to said convention. Therefore let all male citizens of full age come together on that day, at places and within districts to be hereafter duly specified under my direction, by officers of the army duly appointed for that purpose, and then and there with due form of law, select by ballot such persons as they may desire to represent them in said convention. And be it further ordered, that, on the first day of January, 1987, all persons who shall be selected as delegates to said convention shall report for duty in this capital city of Bellamy.

Signed,
DICK TATOR.

This act of one who might have made himself a king, and with the help of the army a tyrant, was hailed with delight by the masses of the people. To some of the wisest men of the land however, it boded only evil, so the author said, for socialistic and communistic tendencies were so vastly in the ascendency that some wild scheme for the government of the nation seemed inevitable. They willingly conceded, however, that the times afforded the best opportunity for testing such a scheme, that ever had been known in the history of mankind.

It would be to the forwarding of this scheme, that all land titles had been obliterated and every citizen held his home by right of possession, only "might made right." Personal property had been reduced by destruction and distribution to a minimum in the individual case. The rich were either robbed or slain. Secularism, war, and communism, had gone far toward crushing out the virtue and morals once inculcated by the church, and human reason crimsoned with slaughter, and red handed with crime, was deified, and there were few left to rebuke crime against the vested rights of mankind. State and national lines were obliterated, so that nothing stood in the way of establishing one central government clothed with military power. Ten years of warfare had made the people used to military control, and they had so long depended on the army for protection, that they were quite willing to submit to anything in that line.

The other nations of the world were too busy looking after their own affairs to interfere on this continent. These and many other facts I gleaned from this book, until finally I came to the message of Gen. Dick Tator to the constitutional convention setting forth in an able manner his views, concerning the kind of government needed by the people. The following is so much of this important paper as referred to his plan for the establishment of a military republic, based on communistic economics:

*To the Honorable Gentlemen, Delegates to the Constitu'ional Convention of the Great Nation of North America:*

It appears to me both fitting, and just, that having convened you at my own instance by general proclamation, for the purpose therein set forth, that I should at the very opening of your proceedings lay before your honorable body, a declaration of my conception of the onerous duties devolving upon you, and to present to you my well matured plan, for the formation of a new republic. We ought by all means to use our best endeavors to profit by the history of the past, and to avoid if possible the evils which attended the career of the old Republic. Let us learn wisdom by its experience and profit by its failures.

These evils it seems to me were concentrated in the intense individualism, and social antagonisms, arising from the personal liberty, and public freedom of its citizens. The possibility of the acquisition of wealth, the personal ownership of anything beyond a daily supply of food and raiment, has been demonstrated to be an unmitigated evil, and the basis of all crime. It will gentlemen be your happy opportunity to bring about a condition of society wherein acquisitiveness shall be destroyed, and the larger portion of the ambitions of mankind forever broken, for want of incentive to action. In short it will be yours to devise such a scheme of civil government, as will establish a perfect and universal equipoise between vice and virtue.

The constitution which it will be your duty to formulate, should provide in the first place for a perfect

### SYSTEM OF EDUCATION.

In furtherance of the social scheme which I have the honor herein to submit, you should in general terms provide for a statute law, that shall make all the children born in this country to be wards of the government; to be maintained and educated by it. Each child should receive the benefits of its equal per capita share of the nations products as hereinafter provided, so that it may be cared for if deemed best entirely independent of its parents. The education provided for should be of a purely secular character, excluding all forms of religious service, and all religious teaching in text books. The book called the Bible should not on any account be used in the public schools. Thus the minds of the young should be left entirely unbiased concerning any religious faith whatever.

Schools of Technology should be liberally patronized; in order that our young men and young women may be well prepared to perform some useful service to society. As ease, amusement, and recreation are the chief ends to be sought in the lives of men, we should undertake on a stupendous and magnificent scale to provide for them. Both young and old will be amused if we provide races, arena contests, theatricals, shows, games and dances and the like; and in these various accomplishments our young people should be made proficient by thorough education.

### ENLISTMENTS.

All persons at the age of twenty-one should be required to enlist for three years in an industrial army for the performance of the duties of a common laborer. These should be required to work at such times, and at such places as the public good demands, under the control of overseers selected from among those whose three years of labor have expired. At the expiration of the three years each person shall be called upon to select for himself, or herself, the trade, profession or occupation for which they may seem the best fitted. For this choice, whatever it may be, they should be taught by the government, and continued in the control of the same, until they shall reach the age of forty-five; when they should be discharged, with a life annuity to be paid from the nation's goods.

### EXCEPTIONAL CASES.

For the sake of greater flexibility in the operations of this army, the right of abnegation might be granted to those who at the age of thirty-three shall voluntarily agree to receive as their annual portion of credit from the government, one half of the amount which would be theirs, should they continue until the full term of enlistment had ended. Also in case any number of people should desire religious instruction, they may hire, from the government, buildings in which to hold their services; and may purchase the time of a minister to teach them; paying therefor, through their cards of credit, by relinquishing so much of their claim on the government for support; as buildings or ministers may cost. Editors of newspapers might be obtained in the same way.

## PERSONAL CREDITS.

Our laws should provide for an annual distribution of the nation's earnings to all persons alike, without regard to ability, skill, age, sex, or to the character, or amount of labor performed. It is sufficient that they are human beings. This may be done by a system of credit cards, not transferable, but which shall represent the share of the individual holder. When anything is obtained by the person holding the card, from the government; then let the dispensing agent punch the same to the amount of money valuation of the goods so obtained. In thus issuing alike to all, no child should be dependent on its parents; nor parents responsible for its support. Wives will not be dependent on their husbands, so there need be no obligations assumed by the husband. The antagonisms and competitions which grow out of ample rewards for great deeds, will, under this system of equality cease to exist.

## QUESTIONS OF FINANCE.

You will observe that under this industrial system financial questions are all solved. There will be no need of money, bonds, banks, or any provision for commercial relations with other nations; except in the matter of exchange of goods, for it is certainly anticipated that all the nations of the earth will at once adopt this system, so that an interchange of credit cards will be all that will be necessary to protect our citizens in foreign countries, or to arrange with those who visit our shores. The questions of wages, rent, and interest, will also be disposed of at once; and will soon become as matters unknown among us except in history. There will be no need of taxes either direct or by import duties; we may also abolish all internal revenue. The support of all officers of the government, and the pay of the occasional congress if one should be found necessary, will demand no more reward than that of the common laborer.

### INCREASED PRODUCTION.

The co-operation of such an industrial army will immensely increase production, so that there need be no study of economy on the part of the individual or the nation. Not only the necessaries but the luxuries of life will be equally at the command of everyone. The government should manufacture whatever is demanded by any considerable number of people. The personal habits of the people must be held sacred and therefore opium, tobacco, and liquors should be furnished as freely as food and clothing. The aim of the government should be to develop the virtue and power of the people, by gratifying all their possible wants, and by permitting no competitions in business, destroy all possible antagonisms among men.

### LAND TITLES.

Land being a gift of nature should not be monopolized by the individual; it is the worst form of robbery so to do. As all personal land titles are now destroyed it will be your duty to permanently secure their vestment in the government, which may furnish them to the occupant, receiving pay for the same through the credit card system. As we do not acknowledge the right of our own people to hold land in personal right we cannot concede the right to foreigners, therefore the confiscation of all landed estates held in this country by foreigners must be maintained.

### CITIZENS.

All the members of our industrial army should be accounted citizens, but only males should be permitted to vote, and hold office; and these not until they have attained the age of forty-five. They will then have leisure for these matters, and would not mar the peace and harmony of the army. The appointed officers such as overseers and bosses may be selected from the army of enlisted men.

### PUBLIC IMPROVEMENTS.

Let all railways, lines of steamers, telegraph and all improvements of a public character be owned and operated by the government. There should be provided at convenient places in the great cities, and along all public highways, dining halls and places of public entertainments, where the people may be fed and housed.

### COURTS, PRISONS AND CRIMINALS.

It will not be necessary to provide for courts except

in the form of arbitrators between man and man. The legal profession will be found unnecessary, and as all crimes will soon disappear with the old forms prisons will not be needed. The few criminals that may still claim attention, should be treated as insane people are treated, that is, gently restrained.

## SOCIAL RELATIONS.

The marriage relation which has heretofore been to many, a system of slavery, will be lifted into the liberty of a civil contract binding only at the will of both parties, and to be severed at the will of those who make it. As women and children are to be fully supported by the state, the continuance of the family relation will not be a necessity; and it may be found necessary to take charge of the children, and raise them by persons appointed by the state for that purpose. This would cheapen the work and greatly lighten the burdens of maternity.

## ARMY, NAVY, AND DEFENCES.

I deem it unnecessary to provide for any military defense whatever, as the nations of the earth will certainly find it to their advantage not to go to war with us, and as such public works would remove a large number of able bodied citizens from our industrial ranks, we should certainly avoid them.

I need not further burden my readers with quotations from this ponderous document. When the day arrived for the assembling of the convention the author said that Dick Tator appeared, and calling them to order delivered his message, and providing them with a temporary chairman, withdrew and left them to their work. The book contained the photographs of these distinguished statesmen, and judging from these and the personal description given of them, I judged that they were capable of adopting anything suggested by their great leader. From some of the country districts there had been sent up a few able men, who were not ready to believe that the old forms of society were to blame for this bloody revolution; or that this industrial army scheme would solve the social problems of mankind.

The convention was finally organized with a pronounced socialist in the chair, committees to whom various parts of the Governors message were assigned were appointed, and pending their reports the convention suspended the rules which usually govern a parliamentary body, and proceeded to a general discussion of the whole scheme as presented in the message of the Governor.

I draw freely upon the fine stenographic report which I found in the book to which I have referred, in order that my readers may understand the various influences which came to determine the action of the body. After some preliminary motions and votes the Hon. Senti Mentalist, of the Hub District obtained the floor; and, among many other things, said: Mr. Speaker: I trust, sir, that we shall be able to rise to the altitude of our possibilities on this magnificent occasion. We are here, Mr. Speaker, and gentlemen of this august body for the purpose of laying the foundations of the mightiest social system our world ever saw. The whole continent stretches out before us without state or national lines to in any way impede our progress. Old forms have been dissolved in the fervent heat of civil war, all legal impediments and vested rights removed, and with the instructive experiences of the past ages behind us, the nations of the earth observing us, and posterity awaiting our decision, we may well take time and care to develope a scheme of government which shall be the glory of all the ages.

His Honor, the Governor General, has been exceedingly felicitous in laying before us his magnificent social scheme; altogether worthy of such a head and heart as our leader possesses. Among the many fine things presented by him I was more especially moved by the enunciation of that principle, that in the building of our social system we should strike an exact equipoise between vice and virtue. This we may do by destroying all individualism in action, all liberty of antagonisms; society assuming all responsibility of moral action. Thus we shall make it impossible to do wrong, and unnecessary to make any effort to do right.

I long for a social condition wherein thinking men, at some proper age, may be delivered from the hum drum of every day life and labor, that they may have time to contemplate the good, the true, and the beautiful.

If at the age of forty-five years a man may enter upon a season of perfect rest, all his wants amply provided for with amusements and gratifications for all his natural desires, what more could he ask. Could Heaven be better. Gentlemen, I exult in this thought of entire exemption from all the lower order of pursuits, that one may live and luxuriate in the glories of contemplation, and the beauties of the exalted spheres.

I wish gentlemen to call your attention to the laws of affinities and correspondences, which have so much to do with the happiness of mankind. Let us remove all the obstructions which lie in the way of their full fruition. Let the envious chains be broken which have bound humanity so long in social relations wherein the full measure of its possibilities could never be attained; and let the captive go free. Too long have men been held by the absolute religious creeds of by-gone ages, which have only bound men's consciences to their great inconvenience, and that have restrained their freedom within limits too narrow for a full measure of human bliss. Make men free and men will be holy. The instincts of man's nature are the absolute guides to us in framing a social system which shall conduce to his highest interest. If we can make his feeding sure, he will not steal; clothe him and he will not defraud; educate him and he will not lie. Teach him that there is no God and he will never worship anything but himself.

No sooner was the gentleman seated than the Hon. Abel Bean Eater obtained the floor, and in a very passionate manner addressed the convention. He was described as a short, thick-set matter-of-fact sort of a man, who had not been fed on angels food; not by any means a scholar, but having a good fund of common sense on which he could draw when occasion demanded. He was one of those characters who dare to be in the minority, on a great moral question, he said:

Mr. Speaker: I doubt not that the Hon. Gentleman who has just taken his seat well understands the import of his own remarks, but in admitting this much I am fully aware of the fact that I have given the gentleman credit for much greater mental accumen than any of his hearers possess. What, I ask, Mr. Speaker, and gentlemen of this convention, has "affinities," and "correspondences," and "exalted spheres," to do concerning the social and governmental system which is to be originated and put in form and force by this body. If I understand our mission, gentlemen we are not here to listen to some fine spun theory on social philosophy, but rather to lay hold on the hard, cold facts which we find in the condition of things about us, and deal with them like men.

A long suffering people, bruised and broken, who yet linger in the shadows of a dreadful night of war and bloodshed, are watching and waiting for deliverance by our hands. I yield to no gentleman on this floor in regard to the respect which we all share for Gen. Dick Tator, and wish here and now to pay tribute to his military genius and to his patriotic magnanimity, exemplified in the calling of this congress, and submitting to it the destiny of this great nation. And yet gentlemen I am here to say that his social scheme as laid before us in his message is fraught with unprecedented dangers to the prosperity and success of the people. The whole matter is based upon certain bare assumptions for which there is no precedent, and to sustain which there is not offered a single tangible fact or argument.

Although there are many things in this document which I might successfully attack, yet I choose to leave these matters to other hands while I deal only with its many assumptions.

1st. It is assumed that by giving to our children a purely secular education without any religious instruction except that which is left to a most haphazzard arrangement concerning church work; we shall develope citizens of such pure moral character that no provision need be made for the punishment of criminals, while abolishing jails, prisons and gibbets. So carefully does this scheme provide for the dwarfing of the moral nature of man, that it banishes the Bible, the best of classics, from our schools, although it contains the finest code of moral ethics known to our race. And how, Mr. Speaker, is this wonderful change in the human heart to be wrought? And here we meet with a second assumption, viz: That the satisfaction of human wants will overcome and destroy the tendency to sin and crime in the human heart. The gentleman who preceded me declared this when he said: "make man's feeding sure and he will not steal." Does the gentleman propose to treat the lower passions of man in the same manner? The desire of man for food and clothing represent only a small portion of the propensities of the human which in some manner must be overcome. Will he feed ambition or destroy it? Shall licentiousness be gratified that men may be made pure?

What new law is this which substitutes for the purpose of human purification, the giving of unbridled rein to the appetites and passions by providing for their perfect satisfaction, instead of the old method of restraint and conquest for them? Who on this floor, in the light of the past, will dare to say that luxury is better than poverty for the development of a strong and noble manhood? Are we not ready to say rather, that endeavor begins to decay the moment it is seated in the lap of luxury? Who among us can say which has been to him the better friend—prosperity or adversity? Emerging as we are from a dreadful struggle in which the very worst passions of mankind have for years been rampant; I submit that society is in no way prepared for this innovation, and that the attempt will only bring dire disaster to the nation.

The third assumption to which I would call your attention, is that all the great nations of the earth with which we wish to hold commercial relations, will at once adopt this new system of social order. But on what is this assumption based? Where is the promise of it? When gold and silver shall be demonetized and universal exchange of commodities take their place in this country; when our citizens shall hold nothing of value except their credit cards, through which they draw supplies from the government, how can they travel in foreign lands where the cards are not current? On the other hand, what shall we do with the mass of foreigners who are yearly seeking the hospitalities of our shores? Shall we enlist them into our industrial army? Shall we take men at forty years of age and at forty-five discharge them with a life annuity? If our system thus proposed shall be the blessing which its adherents claim for it, then we may expect that emigration will be enormously stimulated by it, and the success of the entire scheme will depend upon the universal adoption by the nations of the earth of this most absurd form of socialism. To assume that all these nations, including the Chinese empire and the tribes of the "Dark Continent," will adjust themselves to this new order of things in America, is too absurd to demand a moment's attention.

Complication with these foreign powers will make the last and most stupendous of these assumptions apparent, viz: That we shall not need to prepare for any defense by land or sea, nor any arrangement whatever for military protection; because, forsooth, the nations would find that it was not for their interests to go to war with us. But, sir, this is not in harmony with universal experience. When we come to shut ourselves up against all nations in this worst form of social selfishness, we may expect that they will resent it, and we shall be obliged to defend our dominions against a foreign foe. And what about internal dissensions? To my mind, Mr. Speaker, there cannot be devised a social scheme so perfect but that the evil in man will at some point break over its restraints and demand for its suppression military police regulations. No, gentlemen, I cannot give my voice and vote to this dangerous experiment.

This speech was received with hisses and groans of derision on the part of the great majority, while a few gave hearty applause. There were scores of members on the floor at once shouting for recognition, but it was secured by the Hon. Christian Socialist, who said: "Mr. Speaker, I cannot fully agree with either of the gentlemen who have preceded me in this debate. In the first place I have but little sympathy with the idle vaporings of sentimentalists, who are altogether too ethereal for this matter of fact world, and yet find themselves too heavily laden with the grossness of a fleshly nature, to arise on the angelic pinions of their own imagination, and leave this sublunary sphere to less favored mortals.

"Neither am I ready to accept the sturdy conclusions of the Hon. Abel Bean Eater, who, if one may judge from his name, is anything but ethereal in his nature. His conclusions savor too much of the old time theories of Christian ethics, the days of the serfdom of the human soul in the chains of orthodoxy. I come, sir, to view this matter from a more liberal standpoint. I must agree in the main with the Governor in his social scheme. I believe that an educated people will be a moral people, and if we can succeed in the destruction of all business relations between man and man, the temptation to defraud will be removed forever. It appears to me quite clear that when a man can neither dispose of or use for his own pleasure any article, he will not be likely to steal it. Instead of making fruitless efforts to reform the acquisitive faculty in man, let us deprive all things about him of any value to him personally beyond the supply of his daily wants.

I believe that like the early disciples of Jesus of Nazareth, there should be a community of goods, no man claiming anything as his own, but each contributing his share of labor to the general weal. We want just as little government as is possible. We have been governed too much in all the ages. We must trust men if we would lift them up into a higher life. Wages, interest and rent; the great social and financial problems of the past must absolutely be wiped out, and this, Gen. Dick Tator's scheme will accomplish.

Christian communism is my ideal and I believe the nation is now ready for it. Let our constitution and laws be so formed that all landed estate, as well as all other property, shall at once become the possessions of the government, and then let every citizen do his duty and peace and prosperity will dawn on our land.

The Bible must be very liberally interpreted or laid aside entirely, if it stands in our way. Some parts of it we can well accept, but much of it is unfit to be used as a guide to us. in this enlightened age. Jesus of Nazareth should be looked upon merely as a great and good moral philosopher, discarding the false theories of his divinity, and sacrificial atonement; we should use his example and teachings to assist us by our own strength, to attain to a perfect manhood and to perfect social relations.

Let all property be placed in one common fund, and let it consist of only those things which are conducive to human satisfaction; then give to each all he is able to use, and care, lust, sin and crime will disappear from the earth. As to the matter of education I do not believe in any distinct moral or religious teaching in our schools, especially if it shall be of a dogmatic character. Let us be liberal and seek to make others so, thus freeing them from the bondage of old theologies and effete forms of worship. Let us bring in the new and crowd out the old, and we shall be a blessing to posterity.

This speech was received very quietly, as it seemed to follow so near the line of difference between nothing and something as scarcely to awaken either commendation or opposition. The next gentleman to obtain the floor was a well known leader called Gen. Herrmost. His speech consisted of a fiery harangue, partly in approval and partly in condemnation of Gen. Dick Tators' message. He said: Never in the history of man, Mr. Speaker and gentlemen of this convention, has there been presented such an opportunity to deliver a nation from the bondage of law and order as now. The rich men and corporations who have lived like beasts of prey, by devouring their fellow men, are either slain in the great revolution or lying in abject poverty at our feet. Landlords and land titles have vanished, and the people are free to take possession of their former holdings.

The church of the great imposter, Jesus of Nazareth, the scourge of humanity, is crumbling; and nothing is needed to complete its overthrow but the adoption of this new social order of things. Hail the day when there shall not be seen on any of our hilltops, or in any of our beautiful vallies, a church spire, the emblem of superstition and the strong tower of this destroyer of the personal liberty of man. Let its holy day become a thing of the past, as seems very likely to be its fate. To my mind, gentlemen of this convention, it is a settled fact that if this **absurd** so-called Lords-day Sabbath, on which Christians have so industriously propagated their infamous dogmas, can be destroyed, that with it the whole system will topple to its fall.

Several of the propositions of the Governor's message tend directly to produce this desired result. Take for instance the employment of all laborers by the government in an industrial army. We cannot legislate a civil Sabbath without falling into the errors of the past, wherein personal liberty was subordinated to superstition. The time of each member of this vast army, from the moment he enlists until discharged will belong to the government; to be employed by it, and let me assure you gentlemen that there will be no nonsense tolerated concerning a man's convictions on these religious questions. To provide for the observance of such a day would be a piece of church legislation which we, like our governor, would at once condemn. My voice, and vote, shall always agree with the battle cry of the great revolution, "Down with the church," "down with the Sabbath." Rather let us have a holiday in which all can join, in which the various places of amusement recommended by Gen. Dick Tator can be visited. Let us to the beer gardens and saloons, where true rational enjoyment may be taken.

No part of our industrial army should ever be permitted to cease its important labors, in order to celebrate the mythical resurrection of a Jewish malefactor who, in harmony with the superior wisdom of the Pagan Romans, was crucified in attestation of their disgust with the doctrines of one, who sought to fasten on the minds and consciences of humanity the curse of a giant superstition, which in spite of all this precaution has filled the earth with bloodshed and scourged the nations by its evil power. When men shall be enlisted in this army their time is no longer theirs; then churches will want for devotees, and church and religious convocations will be broken up, as the government can only excuse from labor for purely secular reasons. Then the curse of Bible houses and colporteurs, tract distributors and missionaries, will be things of the past. The state can never provide for such religious education without violating the fundamental principles of the new social order.

The pulpit also, which has held sway for ages over the habits and lives of millions of our race, must be destroyed or rendered impotent. When there shall be no schools for the education of ministers, and when in service they must depend upon some who will be foolish enough to hire their time from the government, they will then be so completely the mouth-pieces of those who engage them, that little evil in comparison will result from their teachings. Down with the pulpit. And the public press also. Ah, Mr. Speaker, my blood boils with indignation when I reflect upon what I, and men of my way of thinking, have been called upon to endure, from an untramelled press in the years of the past. The government, if it shall run the papers, dare not thus attack its citizens, and if it should it would arouse a rebellion which it would need an army to quell. Or, if as suggested by the message, these editors should be hired by a few subscribers, who joined together to purchase their time of the government; yet they could easily be controlled by those who engaged them, so they would not dare to express their private opinions. From my point of vision permit me to shout, down with the press, and up with social reform.

With the public press muzzled, the pulpit silent, and the Sabbath overthrown, there shall come to us a freedom heretofore unknown in the annals of time.

I most fully agree with Gen. Dick Tator in the matter of dispensing with jails, prisons and criminal courts. Of such places I have no fond recollections. Let them be banished from our social system. What right has any government to deprive a man of his liberty? What right to hush his voice while denouncing the tyranny of the law? And just here comes my objection to a portion of the scheme under consideration. There is provision for a government, and officers chosen by suffrage, not by the whole but by a select few of the people. If we need a government at all then it can only exist by the will of all the governed.

But, Mr. Speaker, permit me to say that we need no such formal government It will most assuredly be made an instrument of tyranny. Man in his natural sphere needs no government. In the early history of our race men were free. When authority was assumed by one man, or set of men, over others, then came disaster. Some gentlemen on this floor no doubt are sensitive when this social scheme is likened to barbarism. But, Mr. Speaker, that to my mind is its glory. In the beginning the father of the family, or the old man of the tribe, administered justice between man and man, and there was no law, no courts, no prisons. We must force a return of the people to this simplicity, or this social order can never be maintained. The manifold and complicated conditions of the civilization from which we have emerged, cannot be maintained without the old appliances. It were better to have no system of education, than by one to develop the latent powers in men's souls that makes them restive, ambitious and powerful.

No, gentlemen of this convention, let us proceed in such a manner as to destroy all business, demnitize all that ever was used for that purpose, let there be no possibility of the acquirement of title to anything, either property, estate, or power; let care be forever banished and let us prepare to use in common all that nature has given us. Is there an intelligent man on this floor who is ready to say: "It cannot be," or "where can be found an analogy for such a condition of things." I reply, behold the cattle upon a thousand hills, the beasts that roam the forest, the birds that on joyous pinions divide the air, or the fishes that revel in the great sea. Are we not animals, only of a higher type? Let us establish a social order that in its relation to the past may be called anarchy, but which will be in fact the restoration of pristine conditions, which will prove an everlasting blessing to the nations yet unborn.

This government, like all others, will be but a machine in which to level, grind out, and destroy the freedom in man. If, gentlemen, this plan were consistent all through, I would give it my hearty approval. Its underlying principles demand such a social condition as that of which I have spoken, and never can succeed without it.

Some who listened to this were filled with enthusiasm, and shouted their approval, but the majority hissed, or kept silent.

## CHAPTER VII.

This great debate continued for days, waxing hotter as it went on. It was very evident that the plan proposed by Dick Tator would prevail. After many had spoken pro and con, the Hon. Sensual Free Lover obtained the floor after many fruitless efforts and said: "Mr. Speaker, there are some features of this new social movement with which I am greatly pleased. As the gentlemen who have preceded me have left some of the most important of these matters untouched, I esteem it a duty as well as a high privilege to call the attention of this honorable body to them. For years I have personally labored for the redemption of our people from the bondage of unwise and unjust legislation concerning the marriage relation. This new social order will most effectually settle the question in the interest of human freedom.

If I understand the message of the Governor it provides for the separate maintenance of each individual member of society, male and female, old and young. No wife shall be left to depend upon her husband for support, and if her marriage bonds be irksome she will be in no danger of penury and want if she break them. Her children also will be well provided for, whether born in wedlock or out of it. I have long mourned over the sorrows of men and women unequally yoked together, not having found their affinity as husband and wife, and still bound to each other long after they have found some one more to their liking. The principal difficulty under the old order was that women were so dependent upon their husbands for support, and had their dower rights of property so entangled by law with his, that she would endure to the end a relation which was obnoxious to her, rather than break up and scatter the family out upon the cold charities of the world. Thus the tyranny of the family has been established, overthrowing the law of affinity.

Permit me, Mr. Speaker, to bring some wholesome truths to bear upon the minds of this convention, although it be in the words of an eminent writer of the seventeenth century. He says: "law pretends even to govern the undisciplinable wanderings of passion, to put fetters on the clearest deductions of reason, and, by appeals to the will, to subdue the involuntary affections of our nature. Love withers under restraint; its very essence is liberty: What law ought to specify the extent of the grievances which should limit its duration? A husband and wife ought to continue so long united as they love each other: any law which would bind them to cohabitation for one moment after the decay of their affection, would be a most intolerable tyranny. The narrow and unenlightened morality of the Christian religion is an aggravation of these evils. It is not even until lately that mankind have admitted that happiness is the sole end of the science of Ethics as of all other sciences, and that the fanatical idea of mortifying the flesh for the love of God has been discarded.

If happiness be the object of morality, of all human unions and disunions; if the worthiness of every action is to be estimated by the quantity of pleasureable sensations it is calculated to produce; then the connection of the sexes is so long sacred as it contributes to the comfort of the parties, and is naturally dissolved when its evils are greater than its benefits. There is nothing immoral in this separation. Constancy has nothing virtuous in itself, independent of the pleasure it confers, and partakes of the temporizing spirit of vice in proportion as it endures tamely moral defects of magnitude in the object of its indescreet choice. Love is free: to promise forever to love the same woman is not less absurd than to promise to believe the same creed. The language of the votarist is this, "The woman I now love may be infinitely inferior to many others; the creed I now profess may be a mass of errors and absurdities, but I exclude myself from all future information as to the amiability of the one and the truth of the other, resolving blindly and in spite of conviction to adhere to them."

Chastity is a monkish and evangelical superstition, a greater foe to natural temperance even than unintellectual sensuality; it strikes at the root of all domestic happiness, and consigns more than half the human race to misery, that some few may monopolize according to law. A system could not well have been devised more studiously hostile to human happiness than marriage. That which will result from the abolition of marriage will be natural and right, because choice and change will be exempted from restraint.

In fact, religion and morality, as they now stand, comprise a practical code of misery and servitude. The genius of human happiness must tear every leaf from the accursed book of God, ere man can read the inscription on his heart. How would morality, dressed up in stiff stays and finery, start from her own disgusting image should she look in the mirror of nature." Such, gentlemen, is the method of reasoning by which we have obtained so much power and influence in the world. After years of waiting and working we are at last, it seems to me, to be rewarded with the fulfillment of our highest hopes. We have long suffered in bondage to a morality which has ever been the foe of personal liberty.

Under this precious form of socialism all will be changed. If the tempers of husband and wife are incompatible, let them part. The government will be under obligation to furnish each a home, and, if there be any children, to take care of them, no doubt as well or better than the parents could. The observation of the gentlemen of this convention will bear me out in the assertion that there are tens of thousands of instances where men and women desire to be free from their marital relation, that they may embrace others whom they love better, or who can bring them greater advantages in society; but the inexorable law has forced them to restrain their desires, and frequently to commit crime, of which they would not have been guilty had satisfaction been guaranteed without it. And, gentlemen, is not this the foundation stone of the whole proposed system, viz: "That all crime is destroyed and all virtue developed by giving man all he wants?"

By the recommendations of the message, also, there are to be no courts, jails or prisons, as under the new order man will not commit crime. Those who seem still to desire more than satisfaction, and show symptoms of committing crime to satisfy it, will be treated as the insane are treated—for avatism, in short, which is a born inclination to crime. How grandly will all this apply to so-called violations of the marriage compact. It is a shame to humanity that so long we have robbed woman of her freedom, enforcing by law a contract of marriage, so that once having chosen a husband, she must continue to honor him as such.

Virtue enforced is virtue destroyed. Let men and women be free to love or to cease to love in or out of the mariage relation. The family relation has been lauded as the foundation of the republic; but, indeed, it has been little better than a system of slavery for ages. Let these chains be severed. And, gentlemen, this new dispensation, wherein, through the demands of the industrial army, the public feeding places, entire and absolute individualism, in the distribution of the bounties of nature and art; produced by co-operation, we propose to bring in the day of mighty reform. Down with marriage laws and divorce courts. Let the parties who make the compact unmake it at will. Hail Liberty! thy march is onward. Hail woman! for thou shalt be free.

By this time the gentleman had worked himself up to a great pitch of enthusiasm, and the shouts from the convention and the galleries plainly declared that he had many sympathizers in the assemblage. I had but just finished reading this speech when the sound of carriage wheels at the door aroused me to the fact that the day was far spent, and that my friends had just returned from the city. I arose quickly and hastened out to meet them with a cordial greeting. The team was soon well cared for by the old gentleman himself. I asked him why he did not keep a man to assist in such matters.

He replied, we cannot keep them out here so far from the city. The allurements of the social life of the city are such that they will not remain. There is nothing to induce them to do so. We have tried many times to obtain help from members of the industrial army. Our credit check is barely sufficient for our support with such help, and the law compels them to remain, but there is no incentive to work, and overseers cannot go with every man, and they manage to make themselves so useless and disagreeable that we are only too willing to let them go.

They have no need either to obtain or to maintain a character. Food, clothing and shelter their credit check gives them, whether they work or play; and so they go from place to place an army of tramps.

There is no incentive to honest action. Some prizes have been awarded of ribbons, or laural wreaths to those who should conduct themselves in a proper manner, but these becoming quite general have lost all attraction. The people in the city have a great advantage over us who live in the country. Large soup houses are maintained, where families may go to feed and save all the cares of housekeeping. Officers are there in abundance to enforce discipline, and yet much of the work is done in a slovenly manner. Human nature is the same under the new as under the old order of things. Hard work is not a plant that flourishes in the garden of the human heart, unless the rain and sunshine of necessity and reward descend upon it.

So, said the venerable laborer we are without help and are duly grateful for strength and knowledge sufficient to help ourselves. Having by this time returned to the house we found the good lady giving a more careful inspection to the purchases of the day. She called my attention to the character of the goods manufactured in that age, saying that they were of a very inferior quality. She said it was nearly impossible to obtain perfect goods. Workmen seemed to take no pride in their work. Men chosen as overseers were frequently totally unfit for their positions both in knowledge, and power to govern. There being no competition nor necessity for good work, neither reward, it was all performed in an inferior manner.

She said that there was no adequate punishment for neglect of duty. Hundreds of thousands of those who would not work, or who did inferior work had been "restrained," as it was called, that is locked up for a time; but they fared just as well in an assylum as out, and as they had no personal rights or business that was being sacrificed by it, they rather liked the exemption from work which it brought. She also said that the industrial co-operation which at first promised well, had failed because of this condition among the laborers, and because that nearly all who had come to the age of thirty-three years, had accepted the provisions of retiring from the army with half the allowance, which would have been their's had they continued to the age of forty-five. The abnegationists, as they were called, now numbered more than one-fourth the entire population. Two-fourths were made up of school children, and those who had continued until the end of the full term of enlistment. Only one-fourth were in the army in active service.

This great mass of idlers had become exceedingly corrupt, and their demoralizing influence spread among the laborers like a pestilence. All workmen were comparatively young, and the result was that the finer fabrics were not manufactured; only the coarse and commonplace. These laborers were men machines, differing only from other machines that in the absence of incentive to free action they could not be made to do good work. All these matters were of great interest to me in the line of my investigation.

The day following this visit to the city by my friends was the Lord's day, Sabbath, and I eagerly inquired after their habit of worship on that day. They assured me that there was to be no public service that day in Bellamy, as the city was thoroughly billed for a circus in addition to the regular races, theatres, operas and the like, which were held on that day. One or two sermons would be preached by telephone to those who cared to sit at the instrument in their homes and listen. Some of the subjects advertised were "Highflying, or the enraptured ecstacy of the seventh sphere," and "Low rumblings, or reasons for being discotented in Hades." As I was not acquainted with the ways of the people in either one of these localities, I did not feel sufficient interest in the subjects to take a trip to the city in order to listen to these discussions.

My friends assured me however that they were in the habit of attending church in a retired place part way down the mountain, where a small company of worshippers who still walked in the simplicity of the gospel of the Nazarene were wont to assemble. If I felt disposed to accompany them on the morrow they said they would be highly gratified. This proposition I gladly accepted, and at the appointed time we left the Palace and by a rough and torturous way, we drove onward to the humble place of worship. While passing along through the deep shades of the pines in silence, there suddenly came over me that strange bewildering sensation which I had experienced so vividly, the first day or two after my arrival in that strange place. The day was made somewhat gloomy by the heavy clouds which obscured the sun, and by the mournful sighing of the wind among the old pines by the roadside.

I thought of my home and friends and of the blessed

Sabbath mornings, "when we had taken sweet counsel together and walked to the House of God in company." How were they felling concerning my proionged absence, and when should it end and I return. But how could that ever be. Two centuries had elapsed since this break in my consciousness and identity began. Where were they? Where was I? What would the future unfold. I could not much longer intrude myself upon the hospitalities of these strangers, and yet I had no where else to go.

Suddenly my reverie was broken by the stopping of the carriage and the exclamation of my friend, "Here we are." Alighting I assisted the old people to the ground, and having secured the team, I took time to look about me. The first object to draw my attention was the little quaint old church, which stood a few rods distant sheltered in a deep ravine by overhanging rocks, and surrounded by great forest trees. Within and about their shades were hitched a number of carriages, while the worshippers were already mostly inside, and were singing in a strange melody something like the following words:

> "We come great God before thy face,
>   To worship in this sacred place,
> Before the bend the servants knee,
>   And lift our voices up to Thee."

> "Within these shades no harm we fear,
>   Thy children feel their Father near;
> With joy our heritage we boast:
>   Praise Father, Son and Holy Ghost."

> "Not in the name of self, or pride,
>   Do we within these walls abide;
> Let all our work in Thee be done,
>   Jesus the Christ, the Holy One."

> "Drive back oh God this tide of woe
> Which would thy people overflow,
> And we will praise Thee, and adore
> In life, in death, forevermore."

We had entered during the singing of this hymn and were seated well up the aisle. I was soon made aware that I was an object of curiosity, as the fact of my presence in the neighborhood was quite generally known. I took a hasty observation of my surroundings and was at once impressed with the extreme simplicity in manner and style of dress of the congregation. I noticed, too, that they were all quite well advanced in years, or else quite young; and that scarcely a middle-aged person was present. I was assured afterward, on inquiry, that these people were either school children, not yet enlisted in the industrial army, or those who had been discharged from the same. The members of the army were kept at work all day, as there was no civil Sabbath law to protect them. The building was very plainly furnished inside, indicating poverty on the part of its owners. I was told that it was originally built by the government as a resort for hunters in the mountains, and after being abandoned was leased to these humble worshippers, and the rent charged against their annual apportionment of the nation's goods.

It seemed that the regular pastor was absent and an elderly gentleman and a stranger was to discourse in his place that day. He was quite uncouth in appearance, his lack of refinement very evident, and yet there was a fervency and directness in his address that pleased me very much. When the devotions were ended and another song sung, I thought now the next thing is a collection, and I wondered if my coin would be current or only a curiosity. But I was spared any uneasiness in this direction, for as the deacons did not move, I suddenly bethought me that there was no money in the country, and therefore collection boxes were useless. I learned that the preacher was called, on account of his peculiar views, Rev. Go-The-Old-Way. He read, with a strong accent, the story of Jonah's whaling voyage to Tarshish, and gave out as his text a quotation from the first chapter of that book, as follows: "So he paid the fare thereof and went." He then said: My friends, the act recorded in my text was performed by the great runaway prophet, Jonah. I have always thought that he would have made a good captain-general in our industrial army, as he made such determined efforts to hide his individualism in Tarshish, and thereby escape the antagonisms of Nineveh. But however this may be, there are some things about this prophet which I admire, and the first is he paid his fare. He didn't attempt the "stowaway" plan, nor the "tramp act," and try to steal a ride. He walked down to the dock like a man of business, inquired where the ship was going and when it would sail, and paying his fare he went down into the side of the ship and went to sleep. One of the redeeming features of our fallen humanity is that during life we spend so large a proportion of our time in sleep; for when we are asleep we are as innocent as babes.

Again, I like his frankness and honesty in dealing with the owners of the vessel; for he had confessed to them that he was playing truant and that he feared the Lord, the maker of the heavens and the earth. Now when that fearful storm arose that night and the sailors were at their wits' end, and began to cast lots in order to ascertain who was the sinner with which their gods were angry, and not being able to satisfy themselves they awakened Jonah, and said, "Arise! Call upon thy God, if so be that God will think upon us that we perish not." Here another good trait in this man's character is shown, He knew that he was the guilty one, and that for his sake they were all likely to perish; so he said at once, "Cast me overboard, then the sea shall be calm to you." He didn't even ask his fare returned. He had won so upon the hearts of these men that they rowed hard yet to bring the ship to land, but could not. Finally they cried unto God to be delivered from his blood, and heaved him overboard.

And they did just the right thing. Whenever we meet with storms on the sea of life and realize that it is on account of some secret sin Jonah, or some bad habit Jonah, let us have courage to throw the guilty passenger overboard, without stopping to ask for a whale to return the disreputable thing to us when we get safe ashore. I have not the pleasure of the personal acquaintance of any member of this congregation, but if I were at home I should say, some of you have a selfish Jonah, some a Jonah of unbelief, and possibly a whisky, blaspheming, or licentious Jonah is aboard some of your crafts. Brethren, cast him overboard without mercy. One greater than Jonah, even the Lord Christ is here and demands it.

The next commendable thing in Jonah was that finding himself in great distress and trouble he prayed. With earnest repentance for his sin he cried unto God for deliverance; and promised to pay his vows and go to Nineveh, and deliver his message. So brethren when swallowed up with trials and temptations, when we "go down to the bottoms of the mountains," when we realize that "they that observe lying vanities forsake their own mercy," then let us cry unto God and he will speak to the evils which hold us, and they shall be broken and we shall be made free.

Again there is something admirable in the readiness with which he obeyed the second order to go to Nineveh. He didn't go loitering around the docks to find some means of escape, but "he arose and went." And then when he entered the city he did not go around among the temples of the priests hunting a cushioned pulpit in a church with velvet or silk covered pews in which to declare his message; but from the very centre of the street he began to cry, "Yet forty days and Nineveh shall be overthrown." He may have recited his whaling experience for ought I know and shouted aloud for joy as he told of his wonderful deliverance. He didn't preach on astronomy, political economy, nor social order; but delivered his message straight from the shoulder. He wasn't a bit liberal in his denunciation of their sins, neither did he stop to defend the administration of Almighty God in dealing with rebels. He had just had a taste of administrative justice himself, strong enough to make him, and the whale too, sick of sin and sinners.

Another thing I like about Jonah is that he didn't shorten his sermon to suit the fastidious tastes of some of his worldly-minded hearers, who hated to have their thoughts distracted so long from their bank accounts, corner lot speculations, etc.; for you must remember, friends, that the new order of things had not yet taken place. There was money and banks, and speculators in real and unreal estate. If Jonah were here now he would enter our cities to find the people all given over to play, eating and drinking, racing and fighting; and they would not hear him if he did not amuse them. But Jonah continued on down that crowded street until he preached a sermon three days long. He did not spare them; he did not offer any mercy. It was not his to give. He didn't mind repeating himself; for on every block he shouted: "Yet forty days, yet forty days, and Nineveh shall be destroyed."

But, brethren, behold what that kind of preaching accomplished: The king got down off his throne, laid aside his royal robes and put on sackcloth in their stead, and proclaimed a fast, saying: "Let neither man nor beast, herd nor flock taste anything; let them not feed nor drink water; but let man and beast be covered with sackcloth, and cry mightily unto God. Yea, let them turn every one from his evil way, and from the violence that is in their hands. Who can tell if God will turn and repent, and turn away from his fierce anger, that we perish not." And now listen to the results of all this preaching, humiliation and prayer. "And God saw their works, that they turned from their evil way; and God repented of the evil that He had said that He would do unto them, and He did it not."

But now brethren having spoken thus commendatory of Jonah's work, let me call your attention to some of the serious mistakes which this good man made. The first was that he gave more weight to the antagonisms which he must encounter in the discharge of duty, than to the infinite resources of Him for whom he was to deliver the message. God's way, by a large majority, is not to remove the difficulty, but to give grace and power to overcome. Difficulties and antagonisms are as much a necessity for the development of moral and spiritual muscle, as are the courage, grace and strength to conquer them. God's spiritual and moral methods are universally co-operative, though frequently antagonistic; and however bountiful the supply may be for his children, He never gives in excess of present, persistent, and possible effort. Satiety for any continued length of time is death to joyful participation, and the grave of growth and development.

Jonah's second great mistake was in thinking that there was no God in Tarshish. He arose to flee from the Lord's presence. The fact was that he had determined to act the shirk and the coward. He thought, no doubt, If I don't do this work God will find some one who will. If I go over to Tarshish He can't find me. This is a bad message anyway and very dangerous business. If God can destroy those people why can't He feed them and clothe them. If well fed and well clothed they won't steal, rob and do violence. If they get drunk and are licentious why not satisfy their appetites and passions. Oh, if I could only preach a gospel of gratification to them how gladly I would go, but this cry of "forty days and destruction," will awaken antagonisms and I shall be slain. I'll run away from God.

But God did not propose to let the truant social philosopher off that way. His law makes vice and virtue at eternal war. Friction is the life of nature, a perfect equipoise in the forces of the natural or spiritual world would be death.

His third mistake was in going on that whaling voyage, when he should have been preaching to the sinners of Nineveh. He sadly missed his calling and was "taken in." And so it is, brethren, that many of our people are held in the serfdom of our industrial army and are forced to choose, not what God has called them to, but what task-masters believe they can best perform. Our secular, soulless, Sabbathless nation seizes men at their birth, takes possession of their bodies, intellects and souls; dwarfs, warps, minifies and crushes, until liberty and manhood are gone; substituting for the free individual entity a human machine, on which they have stamped the atheistic materialism of the saying, "Eat, drink and be merry, for to-morrow we die."

His fourth mistake was in being angry when God showed mercy on the Ninevites, accepted their hearty repentance and let the sword of justice drop. He made bold to make his knowledge of God's mercy as a justification of his attempted flight to Tarshish. He said, "For I know that Thou art a gracious God and merciful." He intimated that he suspected that God would have mercy on that city and not bring to pass what he threatened; and this wounded Jonah's pride, and he said, "It is better for me to die than to live." So many times in our human weakness we are chagrined when God shows mercy instead of well deserved wrath.

In conclusion, let me further emphasize one fact in this lesson from Jonah. The redeeming feature of his attempted escapade was, that "he paid his fare" on that boat. He did not have to offer in pay a credit check from his government, which, as these men had all they wanted to eat and wear, would have been of no use to them whatever. This leads me to speak of the law of compensation, as seen in nature, and revealed in God's word. Our social order is in absolute violation of this law at every point. Is it any wonder that the nation is wrecked and in ruin?

In his rewards and punishments God makes distinction in men, both in this life and that which is to come. Before the law all are equal to do their best, and that individual best, is the measure of reward, thus making it commensurate with endeavor, and ability to perform. The possibilities of reward are modified by capacity to enjoy, and when the supply of natural wants is made the limit of reward, it with both limit the endeavor and the capacity. No man has a natural right to more than he can earn, except that right which is inherent in our common brotherhood, by which the strong are to bear the infirmities of the weak. And this is charity not debt. The free exercise of this virtue is enobling; the forced exercise of it is either negative or debasing.

It is a law of God, observed in men and animals as well as herbs and fruits, that the perfection of species and the maintenance of the standard depends upon the survival of the fittest. Law is God's method of doing things, and under the law compensation is meted out according to fact, and not by arithmetical numbers. This is God's social order, this is Christ's law of fruit bearing. Some thirty, some forty, some sixty, and some an hundred fold. "One star differeth from another star in Glory," "so also is the resurrection of the dead."

Brethren let us aspire to the best there is in us, and for us. One shall not prevent another, but colaboring together in Christ, with God; we shall in the great day of our approving like the son of God, "see of the travail of our souls and be satisfied."

The service ended a general hand shaking ensued. I was introduced to many of the congregation from whom I received a hearty shake of the hand. They politely refrained from questioning me and earnestly invited me to come again. Returning as we had gone, we were soon at home; and passed the remainder of the day in social and religious conversation. The night came on and we lay down to rest.

## CHAPTER VIII.

Somehow that night my sleep was greatly disturbed, and I had a singular dream which weighed very heavily on my mind for a long time. I thought in my dream that a strange looking prophet, as the people called him, was preaching in the streets of the city where I lived, and crying day and night, "Repent, repent, and turn from your sins to God, or you shall all miserably perish." As I listened I seemed to be deeply awakened on account of my sins, which rested like a burden of lead on my heart. I went after this stranger, and having found him, I explained to him as best I could my mental condition. He said that his name was Evangelist, and he urged me at once to fly from the city, we knew not at what moment it might be destroyed on account of its desperate wickedness.

This greatly alarmed me and I cried out "Where shall I go?" He then kindly pointed out the way and gave me a little book which was a chart of the road clear through to the Celestial City, to which he advised me to go. Seizing this, I started, reading as I ran, until I came to the outskirts of the city. Here I was suddenly accosted by a very pleasant-spoken, well dressed gentleman who kindly asked me where I was going in such haste, and what was it concerned me so deeply. I told him that I had started for the Celestial City, and was in haste because I had learned that our city was liable to be destroyed at any time, and I did not wish to perish with it. He smiled at this and said: "So I have heard many times, but I do not believe it. Nevertheless, I have heard such good reports of the place of which you speak that I have termined to go there too."

But said he, "where is your baggage." O, I said, I could not carry it with me as the way is hard to travel, and the burden which I carry in my heart is quite enough for the journey. At this he laughed immoderately and said, oh nonsense, about that burden on your heart, you must have been listening to our crazy street preacher who is driving half the people wild with his follies. There is no such thing said he as a burden of sin, and I advise you to return at once with me to get our baggage, for the old way of which you speak is long since abandoned except by a few old fogies. Why, my dear friend, said he, we now have a first-class railroad called the "Destruction City, Vanity Fair, and Celestial City Railway." It runs first-class coaches, all sleepers, except the baggage cars, regular through trains with Eternal Life Insurance policies given freely to all passengers. He said there were days long gone by in which people passed over this way on foot, meeting with great difficulties and frequently perishing by the way, But that was all changed now. These old enemies had all become friends of the travelers over the way. But I told him I was poor, and had no money with which I could pay my fare. Ah, said he, that is the beauty of this new plan, there is no fare to pay. Competition with the old way has brought this about. Those who still go over that road must trudge along on foot begging their way. We go to the Celestial City now by a process of social co-operation, which

# AND WHAT I SAW.     103

in fact has made the city of Destruction so desirable a place that comparatively few undertake the journey at all.

He said, "don't be foolish about this. Let us take our time, get our baggage and go with the respectable company He said that the train started from the foot of the very street on which we stood. This street he said is called "Broad Way," and the gate is wide, so that all can pass through. I became so interested in his description of the way and ease with which one might travel, and also that I could take my baggage with me, that I concluded to go back into the city, pack up my worldly effects and go by train. Having no need for the book or chart which Evangelist had given me, under the advice of my friend I threw it away, and he gave me instead a little book concerning the impersonality of Apolyon, which had an appendix filled with quotations from ancient pagan philosophers on moral subjects.

My friend, who said his name was Demas Liberalist, volunteered to go and assist me. He said he lived in "No Creed Alley," a narrow, winding street which opened on to "Unbelief Avenue." He also informed me that he had been pastor for sometime at the Church of the Holy Zebra, where the Rev. Mr. This-Today now officiated, but who was soon to exchange pulpits with the Rev. Mr. That-Tomorrow. By this time I had reached my room, and soon had everything ready for departure. My friend had thoughtfully ordered a carriage for us, and we were soon at the magnificent Union Depot of the D. C., V. F. & C. C. R. R.

There was quite a number in waiting for the train, and my friend Demas, who seemed to be acquainted with the most of them, pointed out several of the gentlemen and gave me their names. There was one "Hide-Sin-in-the-Heart," one "Scaly Conscience," a Mr. Moralist and a lot of others from the town of Shun-Repentance. They were all conversing in a very lively manner concerning the trip. They were congratulating each other that they did not have to go in the way that the ancient travelers did. They rejoiced in the great improvement wrought by modern science, which they claimed would yet take the place of the "straight and narrow way" entirely; so that no person would be so foolish as to attempt to go over that illiberal, and narrow contracted road. Mr. Scaly-Conscience called especial attention to the fact that the individual pilgrim would soon be a thing of the past, and mankind would go in a mass to the Celestial City. The ladies also took part in the discussion. Their greatest uneasiness arose from the fact that none of them were certain as to the fashion of the hats and gowns worn in the Celestial City; and as to the latest styles of hair-dressing, they were equally in the dark. They had learned, however, by some means, that white was the prevailing color, and had laid in large stocks of such fabrics, to be manufactured to order. I noticed a knot of priests, also, off in one corner, discussing the all important question of color of gowns, width of sleeves, and a lot of other man-millinery business connected with the New Jerusalem society.

While these interesting conversations were going

on the train backed into the station, as it was made up at that point. The conductor, a small, sleek man of pleasant address, was named Demetrius. He had once been a silversmith and manufactured gods for pagans, and had been a great opposer of the old way; but since the establishment of the railroad he had become friendly and was now a passenger conductor, although he never went further than Vanity Fair himself. He shouted "all aboard," and the passengers moved slowly toward the train. The conductor assured them that there was no need of haste, as he had no time card and every train over the road ran wild; but as they all ran one way, with few stops, there was no danger of a collision. It took sometime, also, to load the immense quantity of baggage which the passengers took with them. It needed about two baggage cars to each coach, and several engines to each train.

As one of these engines passed me I was frightened by the appearance of the smoke stack, which looked like a great image from whose mouth and nostrils there belched forth fire and smoke. My friend allayed my fears by saying that what I saw was the image of old Apolyon, who was now the oldest and best train dispatcher over that road. After a time the bell rang and we moved slowly and seemingly with reluctance out of the city, while friends at the station waved their handkerchiefs, and bade us goodbye.

My friend and I secured a seat in the front coach, he keeping quite near me all the time apparently desirous of making my trip agreeable. He told me that we should make excellent time, as there were but few stations on the route. He gave me the names of the principal ones between that and Vanity Fair, which was the end of the Division. As I remember them they were Slothtown, Hypocrite Pass, Love-of-the-World Siding, and B. Elzy Bub City. This last station had been named in honor of the President of the road. We soon reached the Slough of Despond, about which I had some misgivings, but on approaching it we saw that it had a fine suspension bridge stretched across it. My friend gave me the history of its building. He said that they tried at first to fill up the quagmire with tons of books and pamphlets, such as, "The Age of Reason," "Mistakes of Moses," "Banner of Light," "Liberal Philosophy," and semi-religious novels; but it was an entire failure.

After many generations however they finally discovered this plan of a suspension bridge. He said that the great cables which supported it were formed by twisting together innumerable threads of carnal delight, fashionable piety, and pagan philosophy. These were passed over piers of Unbelief, and made fast to the earth by a weight of Materialistic Science. Somehow the bridge seemed to me to vibrate fearfully, and I became for a few moments very sick. The congratulations of my friend on the fact that we had saved the spoiling of our best suits by not having to wade through the quagmire, soon restored me however.

Our train did not go through the wicket gate because, as I was informed, the King had refused the right of way; neither did we go near the cross, this I understood was to save our baggage, with which we had no desire to part. My friend assured me also that the hill "Difficulty" was tunnelled and the passage was called, "Easy Way." I casually inquired after Charity, Piety, and Prudence; those charming young ladies of whom our foremothers boasted so much. He said they were nothing but haughty old maids at best; in fact, he said that travelers over this line had no use for them. Their place on the road was now occupied by three much more pleasant young women known as Syren, Pleasure, and Venus.

Becoming somewhat weary with sitting, my friend and I strolled back through the train, hoping to make the acquaintance of some of our fellow travelers. We first observed those in our own coach, they were very quiet and respectable. There were some lively discussions over questions of moral philosophy, spirit rapping and the like, while some apparently well-to-do gentlemen were discussing the probable cost of corner lots in the Celestial City; and they talked of forming a company to speculate in real estate options if they found the prospect good on their arrival. In the next coach we found the people merry making, playing games of cards, progressive Euchre, and the like. In the next we found only men, cigars, gambling devices and whiskey; these last having been permitted to take the place of the ladies. They were wondering when they gave any attention to questions of a serious nature, as to there being any place in the Celestial City where they could get away from the company of the women and the angels long enough to engage in these ennobling, though somewhat obnoxious pastimes.

We thought the next coach might with propriety have been called the ambulance car, where they stowed away those who were too drunk or boisterous to remain in any of the other coaches. We observed that, attached to the train was a fine dining car called "Diana," after a heathen goddess, who, in her day, was a large stockholder in the road. I said, do all these intend to go through to the Celestial City? My friend replied that no doubt many of them would stop in Vanity Fair, but the most intended to go through.

I must confess that I was greatly shocked at what I saw, and some grave doubts came into my mind concerning the end of the journey. The words of warning which I had heard from Evangelist came to my mind, with sundry passages which I remembered to have read in the book he gave me before I cast it away. All this made me restless and uneasy, and I expressed my fears to my companion; but he only laughed and said: "Don't let those things trouble you. God will find some way to make good citizens out of these people in that country. Let us be happy and look out for ourselves."

We soon arrived at Vanity Fair. I asked the conductor if another train left at once for the Celestial City. He said he did not know; the trains were very irregular in that direction. He remarked that most of the people were so well pleased with Vanity Fair that they went no farther. There was a rush to the platform, and I among the number left the train and proceeded up the street.

It was indeed a gay city: all was festivity and pleasure. Immense dancing halls, public games and shows were to be seen at almost every corner. There was only one object apparent in the minds of the inhabitants, and that was to get the most possible enjoyment out of the gratification of their natural appetites. Toward this end all things tended. A social combination, cemented by selfishness, had been formed; so that the greatest possible opportunity should be given to gratify the appetites and passions. Large numbers were without employment, having served their time at labor, and had nothing more to do but to gormandize and drink. These lounged in the market-places or wandered about the city from one scene of excitement to another, debasing their manhood by the most bestial crimes, and revelling in debauchery and shame.

In certain parts of the city I found the oldest inhabitants, many thousands of them, living in squalor, filth and wretchedness. For them all these pleasures had lost their attraction, and having failed to develop the better qualities of the mind, they were without any means of enjoyment. They had prostituted all their powers of body and soul to the satisfaction of carnal desires, and were now waiting in the stoicism of desperation for death. Many of them were once passengers on the Celestial railway, but had now lost all desire for any other abode, and were too reckless and wretched to make any attempt at the betterment of their condition.

In traversing the streets of Vanity Fair and conversing with the inhabitants, I had inadvertently become separated from my travelling companion and wandered aimlessly about the city. Nothing in all its pleasures seemed to satisfy me; neither did they remove the impressions which rested on my mind from the preaching of Evangelist, and what I had read in the book.

One day as I came down to the public square I noticed an unusual commotion among the people, and I heard shouts of laughter and derision. As I approached I saw two strange looking men, worn and dusty with travel, dressed in the garb of pilgrims. The hudlooms and vagrants of the city with many of the best citizens had gathered about them. They seemed very desirious of pursuing their journey but the crowd would not let them. On inquiring I was told that these foolish fellows were going to the Celestial City in the old way, on foot; and without their worldly possessions. I learned that their names were, "Clean Heart," and Do-the-Right.

While I was looking on and listening to their words with the people I saw my friend Liberalist in conversation with them. He was endeavoring to persuade them to abandon the old way, and go with him by Rail, or else to remain in Vanity Fair, which he assured them was a very respectable city. They replied, the road you speak of does not lead to the city which is "out of sight," at all; and will never deliver a passenger in it. The Great King has never given it a charter, nor right of way through Emanuel's land, and the company managing it are deceivers of the people. They may run their train through the land of "By-Ways" and beside the "Valley of the

Shadow of Death," but they can never get them safely over the River of Death into the Celestial country. This made my friend Demas very angry and he called them cranks, bigots, and puritans. He warned the people to take no heed to their doctrines, and succeeded in raising such a confusion that the police of the city came down upon them, and dispersing the mob administered justice as is usual in such cases, by arresting the pilgrims for breach of the peace and casting them into a dungeon in the prison.

These matters concerned me greatly, and I scarcely knew what to do, being more than half determined to wait until these men should be brought out of prison and then accompany them. for the remainder of the journey, in the Old Way wherein I had started. But just then Demas saw me and coming to my side he began berating these men and trying to show me their follies. He observed by my replies that I was becoming uneasy, and so he proposed finally that we tarry no longer in that town, but that we take the next train for the Celestial City. We found, on inquiry, that the first train for weeks over the road, would start early the next morning.

We were on hand in time and found the train to consist of the engine, two baggage cars, and one coach. I could not help comparing this with the great train which brought us to the city. My friend remarked that the town of Vanity Fair was so near like the Celestial City, since they had introduced the new social system of co-operation without competition, that very few indeed cared to go any farther. **After** a tedious waiting we were finally drawn slowly out and went on our way.

The track was exceedingly crooked, and built on the narrow gauge. We ran round all obstructions and elevations and kept close to the banks of "Judas River," the name of which reminded us to examine and see if our thirty pieces of silver were still in the bag. We had not gone very far before we found that we were passing the "Valley of the Shadow of Death." The road hereabouts was fearfully rough, and at times on either side from great pits, shot out fire and smoke. I became greatly alarmed and cried out in extreme fear. But Mr. Liberalist assured me it was all right. He said these were some partially extinct volcanoes of old orthodox theologies, that were brought into use ages ago in order to frighten travelers and turn them back into the old way. At present he said they were nothing more than a sort of "Jack-o'Lantern" display, on a large scale. But still I could see terrible faces peering in at the windows, fiery serpents shot through the air in all directions. The engine seemed fairly to scream with delight, and at a short turn in the road I saw the image of Apolyon which seemed to ride astride it, red with heat, and belching forth fire and smoke from his mouth and nostrils. I was nearly prostrated with nervous excitement and tried to pray but the atmosphere was so stifling, and God seemed so far off, that I gave it up in despair.

We finally emerged from this valley out into a barren waste known as "Fatalists Flats". From this point the whole country seemed to be an inclined plain, and our speed was greatly increased, the train running without the aid of steam. The conductor passing through assured us that we were now approaching the "Dark River", and that soon we should get a glimpse of the Celestial City. Sure enough we soon heard something like the sound of many waters, mingled with the strangest and sweetest music. Looking out of the car window I saw such a bewilderingly glorious sight as I shall never forget.

Our train was passing along the side of a deep rolling river made perfectly luminous to its pebbly bottom by the light of the Eternal City. On the farther side of the river there stretched away over hillside and plain the mansions of the blessed, the home of the saved. There was no sign of any kind of lamp, or light, neither the sun, and yet the whole city shone in gorgeous splendor. I could see coming down to the banks on the other side a band of holy ones with music and songs to welcome some one to the city, and to their company.

As I looked I saw several pilgrims in garb like those I saw at Vanity Fair, and they were in the midst of the river, struggling with its waters, while ever and anon they shouted their triumph, or voiced their fears. But I could hear words of encouragement as spoken by the heavenly throng, while others waved their hands and urged them to remain faithful to the end. My attention was especially drawn to One who stood in the midst of the shining host, more beautiful than any being I had ever seen. His voice was as sweet as the music of the spheres, in which I heard

—8

him saying, "Let not your heart be troubled," "In my Fathers house are many mansions." "Blessed are they that do his commandments that they may have right to the tree of life, and may enter in through the gates into the city."

I then saw some coming up on the other shore, and my soul was filled with unutterable longing for the reception which was accorded them. Just then our train which had kept moving slowly down the stream ran into a fog which entirely shut out the view of the city. My friend who had kept a close watch of my anxieties assured me that this would soon pass away. He informed me that our depot was a little farther down the river where we should find a ferry boat called "Paternal Love," which was provided to take us over the river. We soon drew into the station, although it was so dark on account of the mist and fog that we could with difficulty discern objects at any distance. There was now a great rush to claim baggage, and to get it on the boat which lay at the wharf.

My friend did not seem to be in any hurry to get his, and finally I was greatly astonished when he told me that at the last he had ordered his baggage retained in the city of Vanity Fair, to which place he had determined to return. Before I could gather my thoughts in order to provide in some way for this new turn in affairs, I heard the boat whistle and the captain shouted "all aboard," I hurried down the gang plank on to the deck, just as it was being drawn in, and looking back I saw my friend Demas Liberalist suddenly vanish and disappear.

I looked about me to see who my companions might

be, but somehow I could see no one. I seemed to stand alone in the universe of mind and matter with thick darkness about me and the dark rolling river underneath. Suddenly out of the darkness on every side peered grotesque and satanic faces that seemed filled with glee at my distress. Discordant sounds, mingled with groans filled all the air; when all at once the great wheel near me began to revolve, and as it did so it cast a flood of water all over me, so cold, so deadly cold, that with a piercing shriek I sprang from the steamer toward the shore, landing squarely on my back on the floor of my room, where the light of the golden sun as it poured into my chamber window, brought me to a knowledge of the fact that it was high time that I had joined my friends at the breakfast table. This I hastened to do, profoundly grateful that I had at last escaped from that ferryboat and Demas Liberalist.

## CHAPTER IX.

A beautiful Monday morning had dawned, and I found my aged friends in excellent spirits. I must confess, however, that I was for a season at least in no mood to make myself agreeable in company. Again and again, just as I would be regaining my usual vivacity that terrible engine would shriek its maniac shouts of derision into my soul, or the cold spray of the dark river would seem to fall over me in floods, driving the blood back to my heart and making me quake with a sensation of horror quite indescribable.

I managed to repress my feelings until after the breakfast hour, when I took a stroll through the great forest on the mountain side, drinking in the beauties of nature and holding sweet communion with its Creator and God. After more than an hour's absence I returned to the house, where I found my aged friend seated in his accustomed place in the library.

He received me with words of cheer concerning the improvement which the morning air had made in my appearance. He soon questioned me concerning how I had spent the Saturday previous, while they were absent in the city, and as to what I had found in the books that was of especial interest to me. I then told him of my researches, and of the great interest I had taken in the debates which occurred in the provisional congress, on the message of Gen. Dick Tator. He asked me if I read the speech made by the Hon. Moses Heartway before that convention. I said I supposed I had not reached that yet when I laid away the book for the evening.

He proceeded at once to the library and took down a well worn volume which he said contained a correct report of his great speech, as well as a general outline of his teaching on social problems. He opened the book and began reading while I listened with intense curiosity.

The publisher's preface gave a somewhat extended historical sketch of this celebrated ethical philosopher, politician, statesman and orator. He was described as a man of fine presence, with perfect self-control, earnest, logical, tender and yet firm in his adherence to right principles as he understood them.

He was both feared and admired by those who came in contact with him, being considered in every sense a manly man. His fervent piety was without ostentation, while he was grandly broad in his views of human destiny. He possessed a keen, incisive mind that despised the trickery of deceptive words and spoke out boldly what he thought. His mental grasp may be judged by some of his sayings, which had been collated in the book. Some of them my friend read as follows:

"True personal liberty lies within the circle of law; beyond that it becomes license and anarchy."

"Out of the heart flow the issues of life; and no reformation in character can be wrought by dealing with these after they have left their fountain."

"That natural tendency to evil in man cannot be corrected by satisfying his natural wants."

"That which marks man as above the beast is the power to judge and choose; and in these, within the limits of right, he must always be free, or lose his manhood."

"Man is formed for co-operation with his fellow men; but it must be "Co." in order to be operative. No social system which forces co-operation can be made to co-operate. It robs man of the essential element of his manhood — the right to choose."

"You cannot eradicate an evil while selling it the right to exist; the more you charge for the right the greater the obligation to protect."

"Men must pass through the world single file. We may not lose our individualism in marching columns or masses. We always reach forward to help a falling brother."

"Woman as well as man, withers and dwarfs, when restricted to a narrower limit than that of her natural possibilities."

"A permanent social order, cannot be built on the ruins of another, which has been destroyed by a gross violation of sacred compacts, and honestly vested rights."

"To have a new and better social order we must have new men. Men are to be made new by the way of the heart, and not by the way of their environment."

"Land is a gift from God to men, and all men possess and use it. It depends entirely on circumstances whether a title in fee, to any limited portion, would be to the individual a blessing or a burden."

"The waste by bad habits among the laboring classes, together with the wicked extravagance of the rich, would support the nation in affluence."

" The utter annihilation of the manufacture and sale of alcoholic intoxicants as a beverage, would lift every home in this land, into the sunlight of a happier and holier day."

"No system of education, no form of government, can be made conducive to the good of mankind, which does not provide for the development and control of his religious nature."

Mr. Pathfinder then began the reading of Mr. Heartway's masterly effort in the provisional congress:

The Hon. Moses Heartway, having obtained the

floor, said: Mr. Speaker and Gentlemen of this convention—The days spent in this discussion the future historians of this country will record as having been fraught with interests the most momentous that ever shaped the destiny of a free people. Here, as the representatives of this great people, we are assembled, at the call of Gen. Dick Tator, for the purpose of forming a new government for the American nation. A quarter of a century of heated civil contests and social friction, followed by ten years of bloody revolution, has left this people stricken, crushed, broken. To bring order out of this chaos, to organize the forces not yet destroyed, and thereby to start this nation on a career of prosperity, is without doubt the chief concern of every member of this honorable body. Doubtless we shall differ widely as to the methods by which this great work is to be best accomplished; and in our debates and conclusions we shall greatly need to exercise that mutual forbearance and friendly consideration toward each other which shall aid materially in bringing about a successful issue to our deliberations.

We may well pause at this stage of our proceedings and ask of our own hearts and consciences the question, Are we morally equal to the emergency? Have we the mental strength, after these years of wasting and depleting, to seize the opportunity to confer upon this continent, with its widely diversified demands, a form of government which shall rest impartially and equally upon every citizen? For my own part, knowing as I do the elements which are in the ascendency in this country today, I have grave doubts concerning the results of our deliberations.

Mr. Speaker, I ask the forbearance of this body while I review the last half century of our country's history; not sir, in detail, this would be too painful for us; but rather along lines of general interest and observation permit me to speak. I believe that in laying the foundation of this new edifice we must remove the rubbish of fraud and injustice, which has accumulated, so that we may build only on the bedrock of eternal right as between man and man. It will be ours to inquire what rights have been invaded or destroyed, and having ascertained them to make so far as in us lies restitution. I do not hesitate to say that this revolution was born amid the throes of the lowest order of materialistic selfihness, and that the wrongs resulting can never be remedied unless we are able to rise above all base considerations, and do justice without fear or favor.

During these fifty years the outrages perpetrated in the name of liberty and law by money sharks and financial Shylocks, on the middle and lower classes of society did slowly but surely evolve the storm which finally burst in such fury on the heads of our devoted people. Happy are the dead of our patriots and statesmen, who fell asleep before this devastating flood swept over the land. The sweat and blood of unrequitted toil, yet cries out of the ground against men and corporations, who have wrung the last penny by fraud and extortion from the laboring classes. We cannot wonder that when they had filled up the measure of their iniquities that God should permit these wronged and despoiled ones to rise up against their oppressors, and sweep them and their illgotten gains off the face of the land, as with the besom of destruction.

But gentlemen wealth is not necessarily vice, neither is poverty an equivalent for virtue. We see on the other hand a vast body of men poor in this world's goods, and as impoverished in their moral manhood as in their pockets, joining hands to destroy titles, and ownerships that they might feast on the waste of fortunes, and glut themselves with that which they were too indolent or vicious to earn for themselves. Their indiscriminate slaughter of rich and poor alike, their blasphemies against God, and their crimes against man, will form one of the darkest pages in earth's history. And gentlemen be assured that we cannot build a stable government on the ruins of the magnificent social structure which went down in the fire of this revolution.

It has been said that the land owners who have been robbed of their possessions had no right to them, and that their seizure and confiscation was no crime. It is said that land is a gift of nature, and no man has the right therefore to appropriate it to his exclusive use. Mr. Speaker, my faith in the being and personality of an Almighty Ruler and Governor of all things leads me to say that land is the gift of God. who by right of creation owns the universe of matter. Now, He himself declares "that the earth hath He given to the children of men." How? In severalty? How else could he have conferred it? How else could men use it? Not directly, it is true, by himself staking out metes and bounds, but rather through society by means of Divinely constituted governments. Under the law of Moses God gave these lands to tribes and individuals, and gave laws for the defense of such metes and bounds as were lawfully made. The principle being the protection in occupancy by title to the lands so occupied, and further that these should become an inheritance secured to children's children.

One of these visionary social sophists of the last century wrote: "The equal rights of all men to the use of land is as clear as their equal right to breathe the air — it is a right proclaimed by the fact of their existence." To this a better thinker replied: "Wherever the man is he breathes. He has a right to breathe. Whoever tries to stop his breathing is a garrotter, a murderer, to be resisted. Whatever interferes with his breathing he instinctively and righteously (unless his life is forfeited) removes at once by force. Apply the same principle to land. Let everyone try to appropriate land as he appropriates air. The result will be immediate and universal anarchy, savagery, desolation." "There is manifestly a difference between land and air. The one is limited in amount, has value and is property. The other is unlimited in amount, has no value and is not property."

Here is sound philosophy. It is and has been admitted by all these socialistic schemers that the government has the right to seize and hold lands. On this point there need be no debate. If in this country at its early settlement by our people the colonies became possessed by treaty and purchase of these lands, if, I say they were thereby "well seized" of them, then sir, they must have possessed full power to convey and alienate the same. This they did to our fathers before us, who having become parties to this contract in good faith, and having paid into the coffers of the government all that was asked per acre lived to see that time when pretended moral and social reformers in the name of truth and justice proclaimed them, "Captain Kidds," "Robbers." and "Thieves."

And continuing this agitation they led the government to deprive land of market value by excessive taxation, and when this could not be made successful on account of wholesale litigation over land titles, then they reached the climax of their unholy war on human rights and boldly confiscated by acts of state and nation all lands to the use of the government, and this precipitated the bloody conflict through which we have just passed, and which has resulted in the destruction of more than one-half of all values in the nation. And now, sir, on the ruins of these rights and titles it is proposed to build a new social order which must become to all this crime "accessory after the fact," in order for its establishment.

It is axiomatic to declare that whatever right society possesses must first inhere in the individual. If government may own or rent land, it can do so only by the conferred right of the individual. The citizen cannot confer a right which he does not possess. If society may act as landlord and collect rents, then society's right has been yielded by the citizen. If the government may sell or rent unimproved land, or partially improved land, and this at a price or value created by labor and improvement on adjacent lands; and not be a robber, so may the individual. It will not do to say that in society's case all share, for the wide distribution of stolen goods does not modify the crime of the theft. The fact is that when the government or the individual makes a purchase of land, the amount paid represents the value of labor bestowed whether on the same or on adjacent lands and the payer is honestly seized of that value. The after increase in value from the same source, is the legal and rightful profit of the investment and is as honestly obtained as that arising from an investment in grain, dry goods, or groceries. If I buy grain in the open market, which by a change in circumstances over which I have no control, or by the labors of other men in opening up a market, is greatly advanced in value, I do not hesitate to reap the profit secured by labor to which I have not contributed. The rise in the price of land is not in any sense the gift of nature but is entirely the increment of labor.

In short, gentlemen, society or the government as a landlord can have no rights which the individual citizen has not conceded. Whatever is not found contained in the unit or part, is never found as a property of the whole. The fact that all have an equal right to all land, rests on the basal principle that each has an exclusive right to some land, providing he desires it and can obtain it. All have an equal right to all bread, because that each has an exclusive right to some bread. No one is under obligation to furnish to the individual adult citizen either land or bread until he has earned it, unless it be as charity. The United States claims the rightful ownership to all lands within its borders as against all intrusion by foreign powers, but if their be no rightful claim to the exclusive use of lands then such ownership is void. The right of eminent domain, rests on the solid rock of private domain, and is in either case alike defined by law, which is the expression of the rights and will of the individual in society.

And now, Mr. Speaker and gentlemen of this convention, what is this social Platonian dream that Gen. Dick Tator has related to us in his message, out of which it is expected of us to bring to pass a social order that shall be not only a blessing to our own people, but which shall be so overwhelming in its originality and so commendatory of itself to the otherwise biased judgment of mankind, that all the nations of the earth will readily seize upon it, adopt it, and a millenium of universal co-operative prosperity dawn on our benighted race. That the scheme demands all this in order for its success, no one can doubt, as its author does and must claim.

I trust, gentlemen, that none of us shall be deceived into believing that this scheme is entirely new, or that its main features are at all practicable in their application to the government of any people. Social philosophers of the nineteenth century enunciated this folly, and they had found it running through the discourses of Plato and other ancient heathen philosophers, as it was in fact their dream of Eden restored, and the shackles of sin cast off from the otherwise glorious nature of man. At present, however, this plan presupposes a social condition among mankind which never has, and in the nature of the case never can exist while men are on trial for a higher and nobler moral and mental condition.

But not only are its details of operation quite impracticable, but the principles which underlie the whole scheme are absolutely destructive of manhood and womanhood in the race; and as a social order would be far worse than that of the old, of which it is a pretended reform. Ancient philosophers, in the darkness of paganism, seeking for that new social way wherein the heart, the mainspring of action, should be made right, saw this dim light, investigated along these lines, and determined that the blessing of such a relation among men could only be attained when children should be well-bred from selected parents and raised by the state; the government being purely paternal, and a community of tables, of families, of husbands and wives universally prevail.

Already the tendency of this scheme to produce such results is clearly demonstrated by being hailed with delight by gentlemen on this floor, who seek the destruction of marital vows, and the freedom of lasciviousness. Of this matter, however, I shall speak further on in my discourse. It is the main fault of this as of all other forms of socialism, that it ignores the fact of the natural depravity of the race, provides no adequate remedy for the disease of sin, and in every tenet denies the law of man's being which makes adversity a developing power, and antagonisms the rungs in the ladder of human endeavor, which aid in lifting him to the highest possibilities of his manhood. There is not a social scheme which has ever been offered to humanity, that can hold in perfect harmonious relations any score of average specimens of the race for any considerable length of time, much less the whole race as we find it to day.

There must be law as well as gospel, penalty as well as reward, and that too, commensurate with the crime. Such is the law of God in nature and only fools would organize a government without law and punishment for its violation.

But Mr. Speaker, permit me to take up in detail the various propositions of this message. I too would join my voice with those upon this floor, who have spoken warm words of commendation for the great warrior whose single word has called us together, and who asks us to share in the weighty responsibilities of framing a constitution for this great people. I, too, admire his military genius, and do not wonder that he should recommend an industrial army as the best form of social life. He has been at the head of vast bodies of men, who moved upon the field of battle like a machine at his command. But sir it must be remembered that the absolutism of military law, with its drum head court martials, and its death penalty, was behind that command. Let all such restraint be removed and men placed where only their sense of material satisfaction would stimulate to action, and the case would be far different.

I think the General himself must concede, as will every thoughtful member on this floor, that in the hands of bad men this plan has all the necessary opportunities to become a stupendous despotism. It will not do to say that when the ambition to be rich is crushed out by destroying all personal values in all money and property, that then men will no longer wish to injure or lord it over their fellows. There will still be lust, pride, selfishness and love of power. And these will flourish all the more because of the absence of the other. Think of it gentlemen. Millions of men and women scattered over an immense territory with widely diversified interests, habits, fashions, and usages; are to be brought under the power of a centralized government chosen by a few of these subjects, who by the peculiar methods of this social scheme are separated into a caste, a class, an oligarchy; and by this government to be educated and employed at private or public work, whenever and wherever certain officers shall direct, and all this without their personal consent, or hope of reward beyond the supply of their natural wants.

This army in the rank and file, undertakes nothing on its own motion neither individually nor as a whole. The enlisted soldier has no engagements nor plans of his own, and for the major part knows neither the whys nor the wherefores of his own movements. He does not know when he may be ordered to a distant city or part of the country, for the government must keep its army employed or national dividends will cease, or the army itself become demoralized.

Neither man nor woman, from the age of twenty-one to forty-five, can make any social engagement with a knowledge that they will be able to fulfill. As claimed by one speaker on this floor, this strikes a death blow at all family relations, and a Platonian community of wives and children would be the necessary result.

The general also assumes the position which was so popular among socialists just preceding the revolution; that God, conscience and religion must be ignored, so that the goverment might be purely secular. The Bible is to be excluded, not, forsooth, because of its teachings, but in order that no religious dogmas shall be taught the youth of our land. Thus it is expressly provided that the largest and best element in man's nature shall be entirely neglected; and all this that he may be unbiased when he comes to years of maturity to choose to be a Christian, a Pagan, a Mohammedan or skeptic. Thus the nation is to violate the express commands of God, in that we are under obligation to teach his precepts and laws to our own children to all generations.

And now, Mr. Speaker, with such a class of young men and women as this, raised without any fixed knowledge of the existence and personality of God, or of their responsibility to any higher power, it is proposed to fill this industrial army, expecting that with a purely secular education, they will be so perfect in obedience and loyal in labor in workshop or field, in storehouse or kitchen, at home or abroad, that criminal courts, judges and lawyers, may be relegated to the shades of oblivion, and jails and prisons things of a past and barbarous age. Gentlemen, it is simply preposterous.

Athletic sports and wild amusements are to be provided at public expense; but Sunday schools and churches and all religious teaching must be left to individual enterprise, hampered and bound by the public services demanded by the industrial army. This method will raise a nation of atheists, and revolution after revolution will bathe the country in blood. We cannot make good citizens with a motherless childhood, a Godless youth, and a manhood that knows but one incentive to action, the feeding and clothing of this physical organism.

And now let us consider the matter of the organization of this industrial army. I have already called attention to some of its more salient features. It is proposed to take young men directly from the colleges and schools and put them at manual labor in the fields, or on the streets and highways. This will remove a large portion of them from their homes and subject them to a muscular strain for which they are entirely unfitted, and disease and death will reap a harvest from the best in the land. Put thus under task-masters at the very beginning of their life of labor, they will most assuredly contract a dislike for work that no future instruction can cure. But it may be said that the army will be so numerous that only a few hours out of each day will be required at hard labor. But in the first place this is assumed, and in the second place if it should prove to be true then this enforced idleness during the remaining hours; these hours spent in public places of resort and away from the influences of home, will be as demoralizing to their mental and moral powers as the extraordinary labor would be to their physical organism.

After three years of such service it is suggested that these men and women be required to choose, and learn a trade, which vocation they shall follow during the remainder of their enlistment. Only one profession is accounted as of any value in this new system, and that one the most dogmatical, experimental, and antagonistic of them all. The government will educate doctors of medicine. No law or divinity schools are provided for, because if there are to be no courts and no business, no litigation and no crime, they will not be needed, and if no religious instruction is to be imparted, then there will be no need of ministers. In all literary pursuits also, the lover of them finds himself confronted with a break of three valuable years and afterward must have his time bought by charitable friends, if he shall be permitted to follow his bent in this matter. So the poet, the editor, the historian, the artist, must wait until he is forty-five years old before entering upon his favorite pursuit. To the materialistic, bread and butter trades, everything else is sacrificed.

But still, Mr. Speaker, if it were possible to work this scheme up to this point, yet sir, I am ready to affirm that no greater curse could fall on this people, than to be discharged at forty-five years of age from service. Perhaps five out of every one hundred would make good use of this leisure, but the remainder living in luxury, as is proposed by this scheme, and having had every animal appetite greatly developed by their physical training, would immediately plunge into every excess of passion open to them. Through luxurious idleness and exciting pleasures, their powers would decay, their manhood be broken, and thousands having come to this time in life without homes and families would wander like a useless army of tramps, from one part of the country to the other, spreading corruption and disorder in their path.

But, gentlemen, another exceedingly weak point presents itself in this plan, which must of necessity be fatal to it. It is provided that, at the age of thirty-three, any member of this industrial army, who may wish to retire on half pay can do so. Now, sir, we are assured that to continue until forty-five will bring luxury, then certainly the common necessaries of life would be due at thirty-three, and the temptation to join the vast army of idlers will be quite irresistible. What shall be done for and with these idlers? The message provides for their entertainment. Racing, fighting among men and beasts, demoralizing shows, and variety theatres, would be the order of the day, Wines, liquors, cigars and opium, are to be dispensed by the government with the same luxurious recklessness as food and clothing. It is expressly provided that the government shall manufacture whatever any considerable number of the people ask, and keep the same for distribution. My very soul stands aghast even at the suggestion of this certain danger. Can any man with a grain of knowledge of human nature doubt for a single moment the evil results of such a social order.

Let me appeal to you, gentlemen, in the name of our posterity, by the love of our country, in the light of the history of the past of human experience, to refuse to lend your voices and vote to such a nefarious scheme. The social philosophers of the past century, who wrought up the people by their social heresies to the bloody revolution of the past ten years, met in splendid wine palaces, and discussed the principles of moral reform and righteousness over wine, brandy, whisky and cigars; while a few blocks removed the bloody anarchists, and low social orders, in filthy drinking saloons, whetted their knives, and charged their dynamite bombs, to carry those principles into bloody execution. And now, sir, it is proposed in the new republic, that the saloon shall be found in every eating house, and the government itself become a manufacturer and retailer of this liquid poison without money and without restraint to the people.

While I have read the splendid essays and orations of these social reformers, and have observed with what care they avoid the discussion of the question of the stupendous waste of the liquor traffic, and while I have listened to their terrible arraignment of monopolies and trusts, and over taxation by the government, expressing profound sympathy for the poor laboring man, and yet fearing to rebuke his crimes and excesses, and sustaining by act and voice this saloon vice, the arch enemy of labor, this deadly Upas of our late social system, the most disastrous monopoly that ever cursed a free people; I am ready to write with a pen of fire over against all their protestations the word, "Insincerity," "Insincerity."

Who among you gentlemen has already forgotten the murderous part taken by this unholy traffic in our late social upheaval and fratricidal war. From the dram-shop door went forth the anarchist, not to meet men like men in arms, but rather to apply the torch to the peaceful home, or to throw the bomb among defenceless women and children. With a brain fired by the hellish flames of beer and whisky, from a place reeking with foulness and pollution, he went forth in the name of humanity and liberty to pillage and destroy. And now, sir, it is proposed to fasten this death-dealing business upon us nationally, and we are expected to hope and believe that peace and prosperity will fold their angelic pinions, and abide in every part of our rum-selling republic.

At this point in the speech of Mr. Heartway, my friend laid the book aside, while we took a stroll about the garden, our minds still absorbed, however, in the matter of the attack being made by him upon the new social order of Gen. Dick Tator.

## CHAPTER X.

Having returned to the house, we could not delay re-opening the book and continuing the reading of the speech by Mr. Heartway:

But, Mr. Speaker, let us turn our attention again to these credit checks through which the riches of the nation are to be distributed among the people. This is the central thought and desire of nationalism. The re-distribution of wealth, the destruction of personal property values; this is the paternal form of government, the dream of ancient philosophers, and the chief tenet of socialism. It is intended that these credit checks shall be the only medium of purchase, and the government the only dealer. It is presumed that this system of co-operation will yield such sure and abundant returns that there will be no need of any citizen practicing the virtue of economy. But, gentlemen, is this possible? Everything the government has in stock is at the service of the citizen so long as his credit holds out. Is it expected that men will lose the love of display? That wasteful extravagance will cease? If not, where is the limit of demand? And when the check is exhausted, then what? Draw on the next year? And then what? Why, counterfeit the checks. There are no laws against it, no courts to hear criminal complaints, no lawyer to prosecute, no prisons to punish. It would only be treated as a freak of avatism, or tendency to insanity, as this wonderful scheme suggests.

And again, luxury, the curse of mankind, would perform its demoralizing effect. Christ, the most wonderful moral philosopher our world ever knew, warns his disciples against it. He praises the poor, denounces the rich, and in scores of instances shows that they who have and love riches will be dwarfed in all their better nature, and ruined for time and eternity. "How hardly shall they that have riches enter the kingdom of heaven."

But, gentlemen, history will furnish us with many

instances of the deleterious effects of luxurious ease. Rome under the emperors tried this plan. Constantine when establishing the new capitol at Constantinople gave large quantities of fine food to the people. Some of the emperors appropriated large sums of money to purchase luxuries for the people, taxing their provinces to raise funds for this purpose. Now sir, the effect of this viscious system was to bring the idle and improvident of all countries into the empire, The industrious were discouraged, the wealth producers felt the heavy burden, while the working classes being led to depend on the government for everything became weak and viscious, and the government was in constant fear of them, and the deterioration of the army began.

What was true of Rome as a nation has been true of individuals and families ever since. Nature herself rebels against this abuse of the appetites and passions. The rich and luxurious are weak, the poor and plain fed are strong. Rich families have but few children, and many of them sickly and illborn, while with the hardy working man and woman it is quite the reverse. I predict that with the children in the schools, the women who cannot labor, the old and infirm, together with those who shall retire at thirty-three, or forty-five from the army; in less than two generations two-thirds or three-fourths of the whole people will be nonproducers.

No, Mr. Speaker, whatever we do let us provide for labor for all, from the age of manhood to decrepitude. Let our people as near as may be cease at once to work and live. And is not this the highway of success. I challenge any gentleman upon this floor, to place his finger on the name of any great and successful man who was not the victim at one time of poverty, ere he brought himself by dint of hard work and victory, over antagonistic forces to wealth and fame. His children raised in luxury will succeed only to his money, his vices, and follies. His virtues will be buried with him.

But, Mr. Speaker, in the matter of finance, this scheme makes one grand leap backward to barbarism. It proposes at once to abolish all money, lands, bills of credit and all mediums of exchange. The only act of commerce would be an exchange of one commodity for another. It seems to me, sir, that it is only necessary to state this plan to insure its rejection. There is one assumption in the message at this point which is so utterly impracticable as to break down the whole scheme. I need not assert that this absurd recommendation to which I refer is vital to the success of the whole, for on the face of the document itself this is asserted. This assumption is that all the nations of the earth will immediately adopt this system. But yet, sir, while we sit here debating this question, but few of the nations have even so much as began to agitate it.

It is expected that this congress will demonetize silver and gold, and declare void all notes and bills of credit extant, and demand exchange of goods with all the other nations. But how long must we wait for these nations to accede to our terms? From many of them we have long been receiving what we deem the necessaries of life. Many of these we must buy with money. They will watch and wait to learn the results of our unheard of social scheme before they take it up. In the meantime our citizens are pilgrims in foreign lands; and they will suddenly find themselves paupers in a strange land, their money and their bills of credit worthless. And all this we do in the name of justice and right.

But what about travelers in our own country. Here are tens of thousands of citizens of other nations already with us. They are under the protection of their various governments; but we cannot accept their money; in fact, no one has anything to sell except the government, and to it money is of no use. We could not force them to enlist in the army, and being ourselves without any military defense, we dare do nothing less than feed, clothe and transport them from place to place at the expense of the government. The government must draw its support from the industrial army, and thus the laboring classes would find themselves but slaves of foreigners. And further, so soon as it should be known that such support was being given in America, hundreds of thousands of the poverty-stricken of all nations would pour in upon us.

But, says one, we would charge it back to the nations from whence they came. But if the nation had not undertaken to pay its citizens' traveling expenses it would be of no avail. Then we would stop their coming. But how? Would you use Quaker guns and paper proclamations against them? But we would make them enlist and work. But how, again we enquire? If these people came peacably and offered their medium of exchange, we would have to accept it or fight the nation to whom they belong. But another important item is found in the immense investments made in this country by foreigners. Already the low rumblings of the chariot wheels of war are heard abroad because of the destruction of land titles and property belonging to foreigners. We may rob our own people, but it will require the wisest diplomacy and the payment of immense sums to satisfy the demand that comes from over the sea.

But, sir, we are told that this social co-operation will immensly increase production. For the sake of the argument only let us concede that this would be true; and yet with such provisions as these credit checks are to make for the people, it is safe to predict that if co-operation should quadruple production this method of distribution would increase consumption a hundred fold. But it will be said how can this be, seeing the credit check is limited to the individual's share of the nation's production. That the disposition to live beyond ones means is now and always has been apparent among our people, is a fact. They will recklessly exhaust their credit and come on to the government for support.

We must remember, gentlemen, that millions of our productions are the results of the labors of boys and girls under age. These are properly withdrawn from the producing classes to complete their education. Then again, all who abnegate their claims at the age of thirty-three and retire from the army; then those over forty-five, with the crippled and infirm; all these are consumers without producing; the inevitable result would be poverty instead of luxury. But, sir, it is exceedingly doubtful, whether when the incentive to labor because of the laborer's personal interest in the result has been removed, there will be any increase in the productions of the country even if these consumers were to remain producers. Luxury has been enjoyed in this world by a very few, in all the ages of the past. This is God's wise providence to preserve the race from corruption, decay and death. And, sir, this luxury has not in most instances been earned by honest toil, but by the exercise of the cumulative faculty in speculation, or by force and fraud. But, under this new system, all this is to be cut off and the wealth of the nation is to consist solely in what toil may produce.

Attached to this is a system of distribution that will prevent any cumulation whatever except in the hands of the government, and to it this overplus would be of no service if obtained, but must spoil on its hands for want of consumption. This point also holds good concerning the renunciation of any portion of the citizens due by the terms of his credit check. If when the distribution is made there is enough to support each individual in luxury, then of what use can the renounced part be to the government. When each has obtained his share to whom shall it be given. If it be said that this may be used in case of a contingency where supplies would be short, then I submit that this is the only item in this stupendous scheme where such a thing as a contingency is even thought of.

Gentlemen, this scheme reminds me of the follies of

childhood when the little ones assume values, making the toys of the nursery or the sun-hardened clay, moulded in the form of dollars, the medium of exchange. Ministers are to be obtained if obtained at all, by the process of the renunciation of goods which are of no value except to him who makes the renunciation. But still another and greater innovation is contemplated, viz.: that all public improvements such as railways, lines of steamers, telegraphs, stage coaches and the like are to be built, owned, operated and kept in repair by the government. When we object to this, as a wholesale slaughter of these enterprises then we are pointed to the postal system of the old republic as an example of the success of such a scheme. But in doing this gentlemen forget, that the old postal system was dependent for its success on the individual enterprise of common carriers, who made contracts for carrying the mails in hope of reward and in competition with others engaged in the same business. These very antagonisms made the service efficient. No man can say what would have been the result if the government officials had been also the common carriers.

There are few men in this nation who are capable of controlling successfully such great financial interests, and they are only developed in the heat of the contests engendered by the personal liberty of growth, guaranteed to a free people. Under the new scheme men would be chosen to manage these enterprises on account of personal and political considerations instead of that of ability. Such power also in the hands of a centralized government would most assuredly become the instrument of unbounded tyranny, and oppression. No, Mr. Speaker, I submit that with the destruction of individual zeal and enterprise, there will come the overthrow of the whole system of public improvements in this nation.

But now, gentleman, I come to the place in this scheme where the ax is laid at the root of the tree of social order and happiness. The home, the capstone of the social fabric, which rests on the chief corner stone of the family relationship, will topple and fall by the removal of its supports. I have been rudely shocked by the utterances of several gentlemen on this floor, who have, in the sacred name of liberty, declared for the license of licentiousness and crime; and not content with this, have dared to rehearse in this presence the vile statements of ancient traitors to God and mankind, who in the same breath deride God, the ethics of Christianity, and the continuity of the marriage relation. And this they do while accepting this new social order, which they rightly declare will end the necessity of maintaining the family as the unit of the republic. Thus Freethinkers, Freelovers and Freebooters combine their laudations of this destructive scheme.

The first step in the direction which I have just indicated is the governmental guardianship over the children. Of course, the mother does not own her time or talents; she is the vassal of the government. In order to maintain a sufficiently productive system, there must be rigorous laws concerning labor. Economy and care will be greatly in demand in the use of labor, as but a minority of the people will at any time be employed in productive toil. On this account it is more than probable that nurses will be appointed to take charge of the children, putting them in fondling asylums for that purpose; for if they are to be treated as wards of the state, what would be more natural or appropriate.

The government could ill afford to spare one worker from the ranks to care for each babe when one might care for a dozen under proper regulations. The bonds of wedlock would become useless trappings if the government assumes the duties of father and mother both. The support of the child and youth being entirely independent from that of the father or mother, would tend directly to truancy, and hundreds and thousands would go out from home under those false impulses which frequently seize upon youth and become wanderers and idlers, being cared for and fed wherever they go by the government. From these the vicious and criminal classes would be recruited. Thus it will be when the state undertakes the rearing of children without the love, care and necessity of the family union and the home.

But again it is said, the marriage relation itself is to be lifted into freedom. The wife, supported independent of her husband is enabled at any time to revolt if the bonds which she has assumed prove irksome. The husband may, if he finds another more to his liking, or more to his unhallowed lust, at any time depart without the restraint of thereby casting into poverty and shame the woman he has sworn to love, honor and protect. "Will not the state care for her? Will it not care for the children? It will not be difficult for her to find another husband, as she brings with her a competency. And my act? Why it is not crime it is merely a freak of 'avatism,' a mild case of insanity, of which a little tender restraint will cure me. I will then be discharged and — do it again."

Thùs the sacred God-ordained-for-life-time contract, is reduced to a system which would become the heaven of the bigamist, and the hell of virtuous fidelity. One man and one woman indissolubly united in the bonds of mutual affection, and these bonds acknowledged and strengthened by a law expressing the interest which society at large has in the transaction, will forever meet the approval of God and good men. I might in this connection also call attention to the result of the frequently enforced absence of husbands and wives, parents and children, at the demand of the industrial army. There can be no choosing as to time and circumstances. Laborers must be sent where they can find employment. The otherwise sacred precincts of home will become only an occasional stopping place. The great struggle through which the majority have obtained their homes has made them the place above all others blessed to the possessor. Whatever we do or do not do, the American home must be protected.

But, Mr. Speaker, I will not at this time push this criticism any farther, and while granting sincerity of purpose to those who are advocating this new social order, I yet must dissent and can neither give my voice or vote to these measures.

But, gentlemen, a crisis is upon us, and he is unworthy the name of statesman who shall be found skilled only in the art of tearing down the structures which others have built, while offering no substitute for them. Something must be done and done speedily and well; or anarchy and misrule will bring our beloved country to ruin. Bear with me then patiently while I endeavor to show a more excellent way.

### LAND TENURES.

First of all we must be just. Let confiscated land titles be restored to original owners or their heirs. If these cannot be found then let the government take possession of them and sell them in limited quantities to the people. Our laws should forbid the holding of any real estate by aliens. The holding of vast quantities of land by a single individual or corporation should be discouraged or prevented by our constitution and laws. First, let it be provided that no person or number of persons, in the same family or out of it, shall hold title in one body to more than one section, one mile square, of land. In the second place, let all holdings above this amount, in the name of any one person or persons, be quadrupled in assessment for taxes every four years, so long as held by said parties; at the same time making it a penal offense to have and to hold lands in the name of another person.

It is not good policy to offer extra inducements to people to occupy land, for the sake of production as this matter will more easily regulate itself by the laws of demand and supply. Land may be a curse as well as a blessing. In our large cities the impossibillity of all securing homes of their own within reach of business and places of labor is obvious; but the government should have supervision of the building and condemnation of tenement houses, in order to make them comfortable and healthful for the occupants.

## TAXES.

In advancing taxes for the support of the government, let the law provide for boards of equalization who shall have legal authority with strong penalties to force an honest account of all values to the assessor; so that all shall share alike in paying for their protection. As improvements on lands demand a more perfect and costly protection, great care should be taken to get a just assessment of their values. Let us at once discard that fallacy of some of the nineteeth century reformers that taxes on improvements are in the nature of a fine for making them. Shame on the pusillanimity of the man who, investing his money in improvements on land for profit, would demand of society that it build bridges, make highways and streets, provide water, sewerage and fire protection made necessary by such improvements, and would yet refuse to pay additional taxes for such protection. No, gentlemen, rather let the owner of the unimproved lot of land, who pays for a large portion of such protection, which he cannot utilize, refuse to be "fined" because his neighbor finds profit in the improvement of his property, demanding such aid and protection.

## FORM OF GOVERNMENT.

Mr. Speaker, we shall do well if we pattern our constitution after that of the old republic, avoiding its errors and appropriating its virtues. First of all comes the question of suffrage. To this privilege there should be three tests, viz: crime, citizenship and education. No person having committed a crime beyond a fixed grade should have the privilege of the ballot. Again, no foreigner should be permitted to take part in our elections until he has had a continuous residence of seven years in this nation, and has complied with all the law demands. This would place him on an equal footing with our native born people who vote at twenty-one, but who do not give much attention to governmental affairs before the age of fourteen. The third test it would be no hardship to apply in this land, with all its remarkable facilities for obtaining an education. The limit of such an education would be the ability to read and write the English language.

The purely arbitrary and unjust discrimination against sex under the old order of things should at once and forever be abolished, and thus let woman's superior purity and quick perception of moral issues be utilized for the blessing of the nation. Suffrage is not a natural, but a conventional right, and there can be no just reason given under the genius of a republican form of government why woman should not participate. If suffrage were a natural right then we could make no tests but those of nature, and sex might be one of them; but it is not, and for this reason crime, citizenship and education may stand in the way of he, or she, who would exercise it; but it is fraud and injustice to make the division along the line of sex, according to Gen. Dick Tator's message, and in keeping with the wrongs of the past. Much will have been done toward the settlement of the great moral and labor issues, when woman's head and heart shall personally stand behind the American ballot.

The next important question is that of elections. I believe, sir, that all legislative and all executive officers should be chosen by ballot, directly by the people, and all judicial appointed by proper and well vested authority in the administrative department. Let our senators and presidents be selected by the popular vote. To guard against bribery let it disqualify any citizen who is a candidate for any office to contribute any money or other valuable consideration toward the expenses of a political campaign; then offices will not seek millionaire candidates only. Let the most effective system for an untrammelled and secret ballot be maintained.

## CHAPTER XI.

### STATE LINES AND DIVISIONS.

The question of a confederation of states, or of one centralized government must be settled by us. I believe, gentlemen, that with our wide domain, diversity of peoples and productions, that the old method of divisions into states with limited powers is the most desirable. It would be well for us to reduce the number at least one-half, and thus greatly decrease the expense of their government. These lines should not be arbitrary, but should more nearly divide the people according to population, in order that the undue power of small states in the upper house of our congress may be abolished.

### ARMY AND DEFENSES.

Let a small standing army be maintained, with a thorough militia organization in each state, let our coast defences be well cared for, and our ships of war sufficient to protect our citizens in foreign lands. All this however on a peace basis, while our government should favor arbitration between nations and the establishment of a world's congress to whom should be referred all questions of conflicting rights.

### EDUCATION.

I plead, Mr. Speaker, for a broader basis of education for the young. I agree with the governor's message in the matter of preventing competition in the lines of industry by children and youth. Rather let parents be assisted by the state still more liberally than in the past in the education of their offspring. First compel attendance and then provide a complete system of free education. As to the character of this education it should be liberal and broad. A purely secular and business education is altogether too narrow and bigoted. It should also be moral and ethical. The religious nature of man contains the foundation for conscience and rectitude and he builds for self, vice and crime, who ignores this fact. The Bible, the revelation of the will of God, should be made a text book in every school in the land. Its moral precepts should be taught to the child. Its revelation of the existence and attributes of a personal God, who takes cognizance of all human action, should be made plain to our youth. A godless school system will produce anarchists and conscienceless citizens. I do not plead for church dogmas nor formulas; but rather the spirit of the Ten Commandments, the Lord's Prayer and the Sermon on the Mount.

I would establish in common schools, colleges, commercial schools and schools of Technology, classes in the ethics of business, teaching honesty and integrity. With the golden rule: "Do unto others as you would that they should do unto you," as my principle; and the iron rule: "If a man will not work neither shall he eat," as the motto of my methods; and then with the object lesson of the life of Jesus of Nazareth, I would develope a citizen who would not oppress the hireling in his wages, nor on the other hand be simply an "eye servant" to his master, but rather one who would be "content with his wages."

Many of the business methods of the last and of the present century were and are robbery, pure and simple. The poor are defrauded and made poorer while the rich are made richer, or through their various gambling schemes, both are brought to want and ruin. Let us not fear to bind the consciences of our own people to an inflexible rule of right for a conscience unbound is like a ship at sea, without either rudder or anchor.

### THE CIVIL SABBATH.

One of the direst results of the new social order, if it should obtain, will be the overthrow of the civil Sabbath rest-day. This must assuredly result with all labor under the control of a purely secular system of government, which would not dare to legislate for a Sabbath rest-day lest it should be sectarian. I plead for this day as a necessity to our peculiar civilization. I plead for this day as the hope of the laboring masses, as the breakwater against utter selfishness and blasting secularism. Gentlemen, it is enough to condemn this form of nationalism, that it ignores these moral relations between God and men and proposes to supercede even the law of God.

### THE ALCOHOLIC LIQUOR TRAFFIC.

One of the main factors of this social problem, ever at war with personal liberty and public freedom, is found in the sale and use of intoxicating liquors. It enslaves the individual and strikes a death blow at public security. It is in its first and last analysis pure anarchism. It defies the laws of both God and man; and having wilfiully broken them, makes of the breach an excuse for the law's repeal. If we would bless our people with plenty, let us save the one thousand five hundred millions of dollars which is worse than squandered on this hellish appetite. Wealth is of little service; aye, sir, is but a curse, if it be used simply to gratify the animal passions. Let us abolish at once and forever the manufacture of this poison to be sold as a beverage. One-half the miseries of our working men would at once be relieved, if the forty million bushels of grain were made into bread instead of liquors, if the time lost in the idleness of the dram shop were redeemed, and the vitiated blood of the nation made to flow in healthy veins on account of the removal of the soul and body blasting power of strong drink.

Is it not time, Mr, Speaker, that we should awaken to this danger. The saloon fed the fires of the great revolution, it was the principal destroyer of the ninteenth century civilization, and already has its grip upon the proposed new order of things, and would dispense to our citizens with the same freedom with which food is given this destroyer of our peace and our homes.

### THE FAMILY.

Let us by all means guard well the sacredness of the marriage contract. The man, the woman, and society, are all equally interested in this social act. If the parties contracting were alone interested, then those who make, might unmake it at will. But the care of the young, the morals of the youth, the happiness of the aged, are all at stake. It is no doubt true that there are many mistakes and much misery as the result in forming marriage relations, but, sir, the inexorable law of one man and one woman united for life is a safeguard against a thousand-fold greater mistakes and more terrible sorrows. The majority of our divorce laws should be swept from our statute books at once and forever.

### MONOPOLIES, TRUSTS AND OPTIONS.

And now, gentlemen, permit me to plead the cause of the laboring men of the future in this country. Monopolies, Trusts, Combinations, Options, and other forms of gambling, wrecked the civilization of the past century, and brought untold hardships to the people. Let our laws be so framed as to stamp them out. The combination of capitalists, demanding a counter combination of trades and professions, is an utterly selfish action, and by developing unnecessary antagonisms, will most assuredly wreck the new republic. Capital and labor should be as one, as capital is the product of labor. But oppressions and fraud will drive the mildest of men to desperation. Disfranchise all gamblers and lottery dealers, and help the masses to earn and spend an honest dollar. Let us reduce the salaries of officials and raise those of professional and other laboring men.

## TIME AND WAGES.

I am fully convinced that a shortening of the hours of labor would confer a great benefit on the majority of laborers. Let us provide that all contracts for labor shall be made by the hour, and the general rule eight hours per day; but let employer and employe settle this matter as the circumstances of the case may demand. Let every Saturday afternoon be made a legal half-holiday, subject to an agreement between parties fairly made to the contrary. Let an average scale of wages be fixed according to the character of the work to be done, and the skill of the employe, by a National Bureau of Work and Wages, to consist of two persons from each of the states, which should be formed from our present territory; one man and one woman to be chosen by a popular vote of the people. They should meet once in four years to consider these questions and submit their report to congress, which in its judgement should enact the same into law.

### EMIGRATION AND COMPETITION.

We should more carefully guard the coming to us of the poor, the criminal, and the discontented classes of foreign nations, not permitting them to come in competition with our laborers. While not exclusive, yet the general policy of our government should be: "America for Americans." Those people who come to us and readily assimilate into our social order and form of government should be welcome; but we have no use for the corrupt hordes of anarchists, brewers, distillers, bartenders and licentious masses who have in all the past been the curse of the New World.

And now, Mr. Speaker, and gentlemen of this convention, I promise to release your attention in a few moments. I have honestly endeavored to clear your minds of the mists and fog which may have been thrown over them by the artful presentation of this socialistic scheme. Permit me, in closing, to call your attention to some of the grand features of the government of the old republic. The liberty of her citizens; the comparative purity of her statesmen and rulers; the enlarged freedom and protection guaranteed to women, the disenthrallment of the church; the mighty charities of her people; the exceedingly small standing army and yet peace and security in all her borders.

There was corruption, yes; there was poverty and distress, yes; there was crime, yes; all this I must admit, but seven-tenths of all this was found in connection with one kind of business and one bad personal habit of the people. Dram-shops and drinking was the nation's curse. But aside from this the Nineteenth century was the golden one of the ages, and the American Republic the most glorious of time. If she had not so far forgotten the God of her fathers as to desecrate his holy day; oppress the laborer in his wages; license the foulest business the sun ever shone upon, and break her solemn contract with her citizen landholders; then still she might have had a name among the nations of the earth, and her flag unfurled would have been still the emblem of liberty to the world's sorrowing millions. Rather than accept the wild scheme presented to us, let us now, taking the constitution and laws of this great nation for our model, correct its errors and give to our people the most righteous government under the sun.

Let us first of all acknowledge God the Supreme Ruler and Governor of all things, then let us make our social system conform to His law, and thereby all may be attained which is possible under our present state. Let us learn to use the world without abusing it, and make this life the stepping-stone to that higher life which lies beyond. With this life and these surroundings, mankind will never be fully satisfied, and yet, the truth must ever remain, that "Godliness with contentment is great gain."

My venerable friend closed the book, while his face shone resplendent with a glow of satisfaction, as though a perfect victory had been won. For my own part I scarcely knew what to think or say. I remembered what animation and assurance I had felt when this great social scheme had been presented to me, but now it all had vanished, and the impracticability of the whole matter was apparant. It was as though one had described to me an Eldorado, a land of beauty, of eternal youth; had wrought up my desire at once to remove to it, but who had suddenly dashed all my hopes by locating it in the planet Neptune.

After a few moments of silence I ventured to inquire as to the effect of this oration upon Congress, and the result of their deliberation. Immediately my friends face fell, as sadly he said: "Lost, all was lost. Many were jubilant over the speech, but the majority were still determined to revolutionize the social order. Great confusion reigned for days in the body, but finally the nationalistic, social and revolutionary scheme was reported to the convention by the proper committee, and adopted amid wild scenes of rejoicing on the part of its friends. The constitution was submitted to the people and by them adopted, and the new order began. Years of experimenting have now gone by," said Mr. Pathfinder, "and the results we may learn by actual observation, and I suggest that we prepare for an extended journey over the land, that you may see for yourself the operations of the system." To this I readily assented, and our arrangements were soon complete for an early start the next morning. We were to drive to the city of Bellamy, the capital, and thence by rail as we should judge best. I retired that night sadly confused and filled with anxiety concerning the trip. I had not been away from the hospitable roof, where I had found shelter on my first arrival, except as heretofore narrated, and felt extremely timid concerning my reception by the people. But committing myself to Him who "neither slumbers nor sleeps," I rested until the morning.

---

### CHAPTER XII.

In the early morning we were ready to pursue our way. I had asked privilege to act as groom that morning, and succeeded in bringing the team to the door in good order for our trip at the time designated. Bidding a cheerful goodbye to my hospitable hostess, to whose kindly roof I expected to return in a short time, we were soon off, speeding down the mountain side just as the sun was making all the east radiant with it rising glory. All nature seemed the picture of contentment and quiet, trustful rest. And yet I felt that the mighty, though silent forces about me, were ever moving onward and upward with irresistible power.

I had noticed while at the barn that morning that the family cat was taking his breakfast off the carcass of a huge rat which he had waylaid and slain. We had not proceeded far before I saw a hawk in hot pursuit of a small bird, which was flying and fluttering while uttering cries of distress because of its enemy. While passing a pond I observed that the small minnows were gathered up close to the shore, and that frequently they would rush forward and leap from the surface of the water in order to escape the jaws of a larger fish who, regardless of the evolution of species, or the possible ties of consanguinity, was in pursuit of his morning repast. Certainly, thought I, it must be that under this new social order the big fish still swallow up the little ones; and the strong in the animal kingdom still prey upon the weaker ones. "And God hath made them so." If it were not so, what dire results would ensue from the multiplication. Only the infinite can give in profusion and stop short of confusion. Creation and destruction act equally without the consent of their subjects.

As we drove along we crossed the track of a very heavy wind, which had a few days previously prostrated a great number of trees, only the strong and well rooted ones remaining. My friend assured me that those which endured the storm, were those which had been tried and tested by a thousand gales, and had thereby become deeply rooted, even by the action of that which at the time seemed to them to be the destructive blasts of adversity. I thought, God has planted the mighty forest and himself rides upon the wings of the storm. "He can create and he destroy." Thus I saw this law, this inexorable law written in everything about me, "The survival of the fittest."

We had now left the rugged road of the mountain behind us, and were passing along through an agricultural country. On each side fields stretched far away in the distance while here and there a farm house with its accompaniment of outbuildings appeared. But as I had observed when first I came to the mountain, destruction and decay were most surely working the overthrow of the country. My friend assured me that formerly this land was exceedingly productive, but it had been ruined by the methods pursued in its cultivation. The farmers who lived upon these lands had no personal interest in them, the government taking possession of the crop at harvest and shipping to the mills or for foreign exchange. The same farmer might be there the following year or he might not. Great portions of these farming lands were run by overseers, who had been appointed through favoritism from the industrial army, and who had no knowledge of agriculture, and who had no care further than to fill up the time and be "boss." The highways were in a sad condition, arising from the fact, as an overseer whom we met said, "that the demand was so great for the labors of all available men in the industrial army to procure food and clothing for the people, that this road work could not be done."

The villages through which we passed were in a dilapidated condition, the inhabitants having mostly gone to the cities, in order to be near their work in the army. The co-operation of labor forced the people into the large cities, in some parts almost depopulating the country. This in turn bred corruption, both physical and moral, and then set in a steady decrease in population, as well as in the moral powers of the masses.

After a rapid drive of seven or eight hours we reached the city. Here we saw some display of magnificence and luxury. Most especially was this marked in buildings erected in the earlier history of the new social order, while yet government officials were taught that this co-operation would make economy a useless virtue. But these monuments of a blind faith in nationalism were decaying, and would soon be with the things of the past. The theatres, shows, arenas and pugilistic rings, and all other places of amusement were crowded day and night with the masses of loiterers. The people seemed given up to amusements, which had been provided on a magnificent scale by the government. Occasional squads of the industrial army would pass by, to or from their labors, but they moved in a listless manner, and seemed ready at any time to desert.

The city we found to be in an unusual uproar, as we were informed that the president had been forced to call a session of the congress, it having not convened before in twenty-five years. Such were the social conditions that the leaders of the oligarchy who controlled the country, dared not give the people a hearing by their chosen representatives. But the demand had become so imperative that they could no longer delay. The nation was on the verge of utter bankruptcy. Soon after the new order of things began the other nations, whose citizens had been robbed by the confiscation of land titles, made demand for indemnification, and, as the republic had been left without defence, it was forced to yield to outrageous demands, postponing the time of payment for a long term of years. This vast sum had now fallen due, and the productive resources of the country were being taxed to their utmost to meet it.

Farther than this the causes which the Hon. Mr. Heartway had predicted would get in their destructive work, had and were adding their part to the general disaster. In company with my friend I visited the schools, especially the higher institutions of learning. Students were exceedingly scarce. Very few were ready to enter college before they were forced into the industrial army at twenty-one, and none older than this could remain. Thousands, wearying of the pursuit of knowledge which they could put to no personal use, played truant and roamed at will. Their educators were all young men, as they who chose this occupation "laid down their tools" at thirty-three or forty-five.

The stupendous scale on which amusements had been prepared for the people had reached the young in the schools and narrowed down their conceptions of life to eating, drinking and playing. We visited a newspaper office, that of the great daily called the "National Expositor." Here was the same blight which seemed to effect the whole social order. The editor was hired from the industrial army and his time paid by punching the credit checks of his subscribers. He had no opinions of his own to express, as he might lose his place at any time. In this case he was the hireling of the government officials, who controlled the subscription list of the paper. Like all the other editors of the land he was a mental slave.

We looked about for churches. They were few indeed and ill attended. Here too there was no independence of thought, as the preacher was hired in the same way as the editor. In Bellamy the Sabbath was hardly recognized except as a day of greater shows, circuses and theatres. The industrial army worked right on as usual. The attendance at the churches was so light that for the convenience of those who desired to listen, telephone connections were established with the clergyman's study. This plan had the advantage of being able to shut off the preacher, if one was not pleased, without such observed discourtesy as leaving the church in the old way.

We were also at a number of public eating places. Here we saw the evil effects of the system in its most terrible manifestations. The custom was to deal out liquors of all kinds and in all quantities, and the side slips where parties passed in to be waited on were the scenes of drunken orgies too foul to mention.

The waiters also were frequently so drunk from being treated by guests that they could not attend to the orders of sober men. And not only men but women also having been taken to these places from childhood, and given in the first place sweetened liquors, had gone on from bad to worse until they, like the men, reeled from the place drunk. The preparation of the food was abominable as there was nothing either to make or lose by the cook, and he was frequently drunk. This state of affairs of course greatly demoralized the industrial army. Drunken overseers were insulting and abusive to the laborers under them, and were frequently shot or beaten to death. The workingmen having free access to the poison, and leading as they did a humdrum sort of life, in large numbers drank immoderately and were almost useless for labor, and became both vicious and criminal.

Absolutely no provision had been made in this social scheme for the cultivation of the moral and religious faculties, nothing in short but to feed, clothe and amuse. This treatment ushered in the age of moral weakness. We found also that licentiousness abounded. The family relation had been largely broken up. The enforced absence of husband and wife from each other and children from parents wrought wide spread ruin. Under these circumstances social orders were formed in various parts of the land, advocating and maintaining promiscuous marriage relations. Hundreds of thousands of children, fed, clothed and educated by the state, knew nothing whatever of their parentage.

Marriage was made entirely a civil contract to be repudiated by either party at any time by giving three months' notice. The penalty for fornication and adultery was simply that the party offended might declare the marriage contract void without giving the three months' notice. There were no jails, lockups or prisons. Each county had an insane asylum where criminals were treated for avatism, they being gently restrained until they were penitent and then turned loose to prey upon society. This action or treatment of criminals was based on the socialistic philosophy that man is by nature holy, and that any tendency to crime is abnormal and therefore simply a show of insanity, and that the punishment of such a being is a greater crime than it is possible for the individual himself to commit.

After a few days spent in the investigation of these matters in the capital city we took an extended trip by train into the country. It grieved me that my aged friend must bear all our expenses through his credit check, yet without such a friend I should have been a beggar. I occupied exactly the position of a foreigner endeavoring to travel under such a system. Wherever we went it was but a repetition of the same scenes of ruin and decay, This difference however was discoverable that tne farther we got away from the capitol the more uneasy the masses appeared. We became thoroughly convinced that a terrible storm was brewing which would soon burst in terrific power on the government.

The call for a congress and the heated campaign which was being made for the election of its members was the principal topic of conversation everywhere. The voters were divided into political parties and were known as abnegationists and oligarchists. Abnegationists were those who had left the industrial army at the age of thirty-three on half rations for life. They could vote but were not eligible to office until forty-five years of age. They were known as the friends of the industrial army, in their conflict with the tyranny of the centralized government. The Oligarchists were the ruling class and were said to be systematically robbing the people to satisfy their own lust for power, luxury, and amusement. Between these parties there was the hottest strife, and public meetings frequently ended in riot and bloodshed.

The demand we heard everywhere was for the redistribution of lands and goods, so that personal ownership might develope personal manhood and care, that would save the masses from starvation.

In some cities we saw great processions with banners and flags bearing mottoes like the following: "Down with the Oligarchists." "Give us our lands and our homes that we may obtain our own bread." "Down with the tyrants who rob the people." "Shoot the overseers." "The industrial army is a fraud." Some very old wretched looking men at one place carried a banner inscribed, "We served our time, give us our bread." Some smaller processions seemed to be composed of a purer and better class of people whose flags displayed, "Give us back our Sabbath." "Restore the sacredness of the family relation." "Alcohol is our ruin." "Personal liberty and public freedom." "Paternal government for children, but self government for men." "Communism is liberty's tomb." "Nationalism alive, is Public freedom dead." "A Godless social system, has the Dry-rot of Atheism."

After having spent about a month in travel over very indifferently managed railroads we returned to Bellamy. It was our intent to remain here only a day or two and then return home to the Palace Heartway. We found the city greatly wrought up over the news from the election. It seems that through bribery, deceit and fraud the Oligarchy party had carried the majority of the elections, and there would be a congress sent up entirely in their interest, that would not grant anything for which the people clamored.

The danger of the situation was intensified by a proclamation, issued by the President; who was reported to be one of the most tyrannical that the office monopolists had ever chosen. In this proclamation he attempted a defence of the pratically exploded social scheme of General Dick Tator, and demanded that these demonstrations of opposition should cease, saying that if they did not, the approaching session of congress would so modify the law as that he might use force to maintain order and punish the rebellious. This argument on one side for the continuance of the scheme, and an admission on the other of its weakness even for self preservation, greatly enraged the restless masses.

The crisis was hastened from the fact that the productions of the industrial army had gradually decreased for years until there was not food and clothing in the country sufficient to afford the people a comfortable supply. And still the government was reckless in its expenditures for amusements and display; it being run by and in the interest of those whose term of service having expired, were given wholly to self-gratification. By systematic fraud this class was supported in luxury while the abnegationists and the industrial army were reduced to penury. These men also became haughty and insolent to those they called their inferiors with whom they would not associate on terms of equality, treating the new recruits in the industrial army like slaves. All this and much more which I cannot now relate, had led to a climax, the danger of which we saw on reaching the city.

It appeared that during the week preceding our

arrival, hundreds of thousands of clamorous and infuriated men had poured into the city from all parts of the nation. They thronged the streets and marched in vast processions both day and night. The eating houses were crowded with them and vast stores of liquors were consumed until the whole mass seemed besotted and ready for any desperate deed. The impending outbreak became so manifest on the second day, that at its close my friend and I determined that we would leave early the next morning for home. We found nothing here congenial and my curiosity to see for myself the workings of communism had been fully satisfied.

We retired that night in as secluded a place as we could find, and quite early. Committing ourselves to our kind Heavenly Father's care we soon fell asleep regardless of the great commotion without. I think it must have been near the hour of midnight when we were awakened by loud calls of FIRE! FIRE! We arose quickly and looking from our window saw that the city was as light as day. Great clouds of smoke and flame seemed rolling up from all directions. Hastily dressing we passed down to the street. Here the scene beggared description. As far down the street in either direction as one could see, vast masses of people struggled to escape impending death. Horses and vehicles of every description thronged the way, while scores were being trampled to the earth.

We were informed that the city had been set on fire by an army of drunken tramps, and so far as could be ascertained they had fired it all around, intending to cut off all escape. In order that we might better assure ourselves of the situation and discover a way of escape, if possible, we passed by an unfrequented way, with which my friend was acquainted, to a lofty observatory, from the top of which we could view the whole city. Once at the top of this what wonders met our eyes. In front, to the right, to the left, and behind us in all directions a sea of fire. In one magnificent circle, unbroken at any point so far as we could observe, rolled the blood-red billows in fearful splendor. Occasionally great explosions would occur which made the very city tremble, and brought terror to the stoutest hearts within it. In the streets below all was confusion and uproar. Each seeking only his or her own safety shouted and shrieked, cursed and prayed by turns, while enfuriated beasts dashed through the masses of people crushing them beneath their iron hoofs.

A heavy gale had sprung up from the south, which, while it wonderfully increased the rapidity of the flames from that direction, served to greatly weaken their approach from the north. We could see that the great mass of the people were moving in that direction, headed by the government officials and a vast number of gentry in carriages. We hastened down and joined in the flight. I was greatly alarmed, but my venerable friend was calm and full of words of encouragement and hope. He said, "I think we can pass through on that side with the wind so greatly in our favor." But when we joined the throng we found that we could move along but very slowly.

## AND WHAT I SAW. 169

Sometimes for an hour we did not gain at all. A river ran through the city north of us, and the bridges were so thronged that passage was all but impossible. For hours we struggled on. The sun was now up and the fury of the gale had greatly increased. To make matters more desperate the drunken rioters who had fired the city met the fleeing masses at the fire limits on the north, and engaging in conflict with them, beating, shooting and forcing them backward, until in the smoke and confusion they succeeded in completely blockading the streets which offered any hope of escape. Thus the day wore slowly on. We could hear and see the mighty struggle in advance of us, while behind the ocean of flame was constantly advancing. The sun went down but his light was not missed. His last beams fell on tens of thousands of upturned human faces, whose eyes should never behold his rising. At this time a very tornado seemed to have seized the flames. The atmosphere became most unbearably hot, as the roaring destroyer was not more than one-quarter mile distant.

I looked up once more inquiringly into the face of my friend. There came over his countenance a seraphic glow of peace which no system of philosophy could ever impart to its disciples. He said, "I think now there is no escape for us. We must die. If I might only kiss my dear companion a farewell my greatest desire would be gratified. God's chosen prophet ascended in a chariot of fire, and I am ready for the horsemen." After a moment of silence he said, "Perhaps this day's holocaust may be the price of the redemption of my country and people from the

Godless, Atheistic and inhuman bondage of this communistic social order- If so it will not be in vain. I am ready to be offered up. Be courageous my friend. We shall soon meet our blessed Lord and receive our crown. Death is but the gate to endless joy, and we are at the portal."

The grand faith, sublime contempt of death, and unselfish thoughts of his country, of the old man greatly nerved me for the fiery ordeal. By this time we had been crowded by the vast multitude into a little niche in the side of a very large edifice, from which there seemed no chance of escape. We realized by the rolling of the smoke over the street above us, that the "flood of devouring flame," was only a few rods away. Suddenly there was a heart rending outcry from the thousands who stood in the street as they saw the fire in its mad career, leap on to the roof of this their last protection. Minutes seemed like hours. The black volumes of smoke settling down upon us drew the death-cap over every face, hiding even the light of the flames. Thus stifled and moaning we waited the summons of death. In that moment what maddening thoughts rushed through my mind. I seemed to remember every act of my life, and to have all concentrated in a singe moment. The faces of my dear ones seemed actually to appear before me, and I longed to speak to them and say them an affectionate good-bye. I could not see my friend but I still clung to him frantically. The smoke was so stifling and the heat so intense that we could not speak. There was a peculiar tremor of the walls against which we leaned, an awful crash as the great roof of the building fell, while out of the lower windows leaped the long tongues of flame.

Our clothes were now taking fire and the skin was shrivelling with the heat. My aged friend sank down dying, and with him I fell to the ground. Suddenly I felt a violent shake, as though some one had seized me by the shoulder, and I heard the voice of my dear wife saying excitedly, "Husband! Husband! Wake up. You must be having a horrid nightmare." Opening my eyes on the nineteenth century, I replied with true Yankee instinct, I guess so.

# Utopian Literature

AN ARNO PRESS/NEW YORK TIMES COLLECTION

Adams, Frederick Upham.
**President John Smith;** The Story of a Peaceful Revolution. 1897.

Bird, Arthur.
**Looking Forward:** A Dream of the United States of the Americas in 1999. 1899.

[Blanchard, Calvin.]
**The Art of Real Pleasure.** 1864.

Brinsmade, Herman Hine.
**Utopia Achieved:** A Novel of the Future. 1912.

Caryl, Charles W.
**New Era.** 1897.

Chavannes, Albert.
**The Future Commonwealth.** 1892.

Child, William Stanley.
**The Legal Revolution of 1902.** 1898.

Collens, T. Wharton.
**Eden of Labor;** or, The Christian Utopia. 1876.

Cowan, James.
**Daybreak.** A Romance of an Old World. 1896. 2nd ed.

Craig, Alexander.
**Ionia;** Land of Wise Men and Fair Women. 1898.

Daniel, Charles S.
**AI: A Social Vision.** 1892.

Devinne, Paul.
**The Day of Prosperity:** A Vision of the Century to Come. 1902.

Edson, Milan C.
**Solaris Farm.** 1900.

Fuller, Alvarado M.
**A. D. 2000.** 1890.

Geissler, Ludwig A.
**Looking Beyond.** 1891.

Hale, Edward Everett.
**How They Lived in Hampton.** 1888.

Hale, Edward Everett.
**Sybaris and Other Homes.** 1869.

Harris, W. S.
**Life in a Thousand Worlds.** 1905.

Henry, W. O.
**Equitania.** 1914.

Hicks, Granville, with Richard M. Bennett.
**The First to Awaken.** 1940.

Lewis, Arthur O., editor
**American Utopias:** Selected Short Fiction. 1790–1954.

McGrady, Thomas.
**Beyond the Black Ocean.** 1901.

Mendes H. Pereira.
**Looking Ahead.** 1899.

Michaelis, Richard.
**Looking Further Forward.** An Answer to *Looking Backward* by Edward Bellamy. 1890.

Moore, David A.
**The Age of Progress.** 1856.

Noto, Cosimo.
**The Ideal City.** 1903.

Olerich, Henry.
**A Cityless and Countryless World.** 1893.

Parry, David M.
**The Scarlet Empire.** 1906.

Peck, Bradford.
**The World a Department Store.** 1900.

Reitmeister, Louis Aaron.
**If Tomorrow Comes.** 1934.

Roberts, J. W.
**Looking Within.** 1893.

Rosewater, Frank.
**'96; A Romance of Utopia.** 1894.

Satterlee, W. W.
**Looking Backward and What I Saw.** 2nd ed. 1890.

Schindler, Solomon.
**Young West;** A Sequel to Edward Bellamy's Celebrated Novel "Looking Backward." 1894.

Smith, Titus K.
**Altruria.** 1895.

Steere, C. A.
**When Things Were Doing.** 1908.

Taylor, William Alexander.
**Intermere.** 1901.

Thiusen, Ismar.
**The Diothas,** or, A Far Look Ahead. 1883.

Vinton, Arthur Dudley.
**Looking Further Backward.** 1890.

Wooldridge, C. W.
**Perfecting the Earth.** 1902.

Wright, Austin Tappan.
**Islandia.** 1942.